Building School-to-Work Programs

Building School-to-Work Programs

Strategies for Youth with Special Needs

· ·

Michael R. Benz
and
Lauren E. Lindstrom

pro·ed

8700 Shoal Creek Boulevard
Austin, Texas 78757-6897

pro·ed

This book is designed in Avant Garde and Goudy.

Production Manager: Alan Grimes
Production Coordinator: Karen Swain
Managing Editor: Tracy Sergo
Art Director: Thomas Barkley
Reprints Buyer: Alicia Woods
Editor: Margaret Nardecchia
Editorial Assistant: Claudette Landry
Editorial Assistant: Suzi Hunn

Printed in the United States of America

1   2   3   4   5   6   7   8   9   10   01   00   99   98   97

Contents

Chapter 3

Creating Employment Opportunities for Youth

Chapter 4

Providing Youth with Postprogram Placement and Follow-up Services

Preface

The ideas and strategies included in this book are based on our work over the past 6 years to design, develop, and implement the Youth Transition Program (YTP) throughout Oregon. The YTP is an interagency model of service delivery developed to address the school-to-work transition needs of students with disabilities and other special needs. The YTP was developed collaboratively—and continues to be managed jointly—by the Oregon Vocational Rehabilitation Division, the Oregon Department of Education, and the University of Oregon. At the time of this writing the YTP has been implemented in *two thirds* of Oregon's high school districts, and in local communities that represent the diversity of urban, suburban, and rural communities statewide. To date, the YTP has served approximately 1,800 students with disabilities and other special needs (e.g., students identified as at risk of dropping out of school, or school dropouts who are unemployed or underemployed). Participating students have entered the program experiencing low academic skills, poor social and independent living skills, limited or negative job experiences, and various other obstacles (e.g., history of substance abuse, previous record of arrest/incarceration, parenting responsibilities, difficult or unstable living situation) that can limit life's opportunities.

The goal of the YTP is to improve participants' postschool outcomes and prepare them for meaningful competitive employment or career-related postsecondary education. The YTP provides services to students beginning while they are in high school and continuing during the early transition years after leaving school. Through the YTP students receive (a) transition planning focused on postschool goals and self-determination, and help to coordinate school plans with relevant adult agencies such as vocational rehabilitation; (b) instruction in academic, vocational, independent living, and personal–social content areas, and help to stay in school and obtain an appropriate completion document; (c) paid job training while in the program, and assistance to secure employment or enter postsecondary education/training upon leaving the program; and (d) follow-up support services for up to 2 years after leaving the program, provided on an as-needed basis, to help students negotiate the vagaries of the transition years more effectively and build on the successes they have already achieved.

Several evaluations of the YTP have been conducted over the past 6 years, including evaluations by two external groups. Collectively they document that students' employment and educational outcomes improved signifi-cantly after participation in the YTP, that these gains were maintained for 2 years after leaving the program, and that participants' outcomes exceeded those achieved by different comparison groups of students who did not partic-ipate in the YTP. In 1994, the YTP was selected as an exemplary school-to-work transition program by the Academy for Educational Development's National Institute for Work and Learning (AED/NIWL). Under contract from the Office of Educational Research and Innovation, U.S. Department of Education, AED/NIWL reviewed over 200 programs nationwide. The YTP was one of 14 selected for national recognition. Of these 14 programs, only two addressed the needs of students with disabilities, and the YTP was the *only* program attempting to build a school-to-work program on a *statewide* basis. In a separate evaluation process conducted later in 1994, the YTP was reviewed by a national panel of evaluation experts and validated as an exemplary school-to-work program by the Program Effectiveness Panel within the Office of Education Research and Innovation, U.S. Department of Education.

Acknowledgments

The successes enjoyed by the YTP are the result of the collective wisdom and dedicated efforts of many individuals. To them we offer thanks. These talented and creative people deserve far more recognition than is possible here.

- To our colleagues at the Oregon Department of Education who consistently provide insight and guidance on how schools can become better places of learning and support for students, especially Karen Brazeau, Peter FitzGerald, Brigid Flannery, Ray Rothstrom, and Roz Slovic.

- To our colleagues at the Oregon Vocational Rehabilitation Division who demonstrate in countless ways large and small that schools and adult agencies can be partners in the support of students in transition, especially Mark Barrall, Bill Brown, Tim Latta, Lynnae Rutledge, and Joil Southwell.

- To our colleagues at the University of Oregon who over the years have provided a vision and dedication to quality programs for youth that inspires and sustains us, especially Mike Bullis, Jeri Dickinson, Bonnie Doren, Andy Halpern, Cindy Herr, Peter FitzGerald, Deborah Johnson, Mike Johnson, and Roma Powis. Special thanks to Andy, Deb, and Mike J. for your invaluable contributions to the YTP over the years.

- To the school and rehabilitation staff, students, parents, and employers in local YTP sites across the state who demonstrate daily that anything and everything is possible when talented, creative, and dedicated people share a common vision.

Personal thanks go to Andy Halpern and Mike Bullis for reviewing earlier drafts of this book. Last, but certainly not least, thanks go to our families who had to put up with us while this book was being written—Joan, Jake, Sarah, Amanda, and Hank and Dana, Jordan, and Zoe. One final note. One of us had a child participating in one version of a school-to-work program (a career academy) and going through the school-to-community transition process as this book was being written. Jake, thanks for showing me the power that can be unleashed when young people are allowed to dream about their future, the importance of communication and support in the pursuit of those dreams, and the value of patience and perseverance when doubts arise and detours occur.

CHAPTER 1

. . . .

Overview of School-to-Work Programs for Youth with Special Needs

. . . .

This is a book for practitioners. It is written for the many individuals across the country who are responsible on a daily basis for developing and implementing school-to-work programs in local school districts and communities. This book was created for two reasons. First, we believe strongly that school-to-work programs should serve *all* youth. All youth—whether they have special needs or not—require and deserve opportunities to participate in school-to-work transition programs that provide them with a more meaningful education and prepare them for a brighter future. At the same time, we know there are many youth in local communities with needs that exceed the type, intensity, and duration of services typically associated with school-to-work programs. The additional support needs of these youth must be addressed if they are to benefit from school-to-work efforts. We have seen many students grow and prosper when exposed to quality school-to-work programs, including students who encountered substantial personal, family, and educational barriers to success.

Second, our experiences helping school and community agency staff build school-to-work programs in communities across Oregon over the past 6 years lead us to conclude that local staff desire and need effective ideas and strategies to make their tasks more successful and less time-intensive. The ideas and strategies included in this book are based on the collective experiences of hundreds of school and community agency staff associated with the Oregon Youth Transition Program (YTP). These ideas and strategies have been used, tested, revised, and reused by school and community staff in urban and rural communities across Oregon. The general employment and continuing education prospects for youth in these communities varied considerably, ranging from expansive to nonexistent. The youth

1

served by these programs have included students with disabilities, and students who were at risk of school and community failure due to a variety of personal, family, and environmental factors. Some local communities have used the structure and procedures of the Youth Transition Program to build school-to-work programs for the general population of students.

That having been said, we do not claim that this book is the definitive work on building collaborative school-to-work programs. Quality school-to-work programs do not exist in books. They exist in the hearts and minds of local people—school and community staff, families, students, employers, and other community members—who are keenly aware of students' needs and strongly committed to providing programs that meet those needs. A hallmark of these individuals is their creativity—their willingness to explore and use a variety of resources in the pursuit of their efforts. We hope you will find the ideas and strategies in this book to be useful and usable. Adopt, adapt, or revise these materials to meet the needs of your students.

In order to set a context for the materials in this book, in the remainder of this chapter we will describe: (a) the background and need for collaborative school-to-work programs; (b) the purposes and components of school-to-work programs, including research on the applicability of these components for students with disabilities and other special needs; and (c) the guiding principles for the ideas and strategies included in the book.

BACKGROUND AND NEED FOR SCHOOL-TO-WORK PROGRAMS

Improving the quality of the public schools, the readiness of school leavers, and the competitiveness of the workforce have been highly visible national priorities for several years. The impetus for these efforts can be traced to national reports (e.g., National Center on Education and the Economy, 1990; U.S. Department of Labor, 1991; William T. Grant Foundation, 1988) documenting: (a) the changing nature of the workplace and the increasing demand for employees that possess both solid academic and occupational skills, (b) the growing number of students leaving school without these skills, and (c) the failure of the traditional high school curriculum to address these issues for the vast majority of students who are not primarily college-bound.

Concerns about the quality of school programs and postschool outcomes experienced by students with disabilities and other special needs can be traced to follow-up studies conducted in the past two decades (e.g., Fardig, Algozzine, Schwartz, Hensel, & Westling, 1985; Hasazi, Gordon, & Roe, 1985; Horn, O'Donnell, & Vitulano, 1983; Mithaug, Horiuchi, & Fanning, 1985; Wagner, D'Amico, Marder, Newman, & Blackorby, 1992; Wagner, Newman, D'Amico, Jay, Butler-Nalin, Marder, & Cox, 1991). Although the specific findings have varied somewhat from study to study, the collection of studies portrays a consistently discouraging picture of the postschool experiences of young adults with disabilities, including: (a) high dropout rates; (b) high unemployment/underemployment rates; (c) low postsecondary education participation rates; and (d) large numbers of young people who are basically unengaged in any productive activities, or even worse are getting into trouble with the law. The outcomes experienced by young adults with disabilities are considerably worse than those experienced by young people without disabilities (Marder & D'Amico, 1992). Further, a recent nationwide study (National Organization on Disability, 1994) documents that the employment and other life opportunities of working-aged adults with disabilities (ages 16 to 64) remain discouraging. This study found that two-thirds of adults with disabilities were unemployed. Only 20% of the adults in this study were working full-time, with another 11% working part-time. Fully 79% of the unemployed adults (84% of those 16 to 44 years of age) indicated that they wanted a job.

States and local communities across the country are attempting to respond to these issues through a combination of federal and state initiatives and local ingenuity. Literally hundreds of training, research, and demonstration projects have been implemented in states and communities over the past 15 years to understand and improve the school programs and transition services available to students with disabilities (Rusch, Kohler, & Hughes, 1992). Although much remains to be done, much has been learned about effective and promising school and transition practices that will improve the outcomes of youth with disabilities. The increasing groundswell of interest has also resulted in federal initiatives aimed at improving school programs and student outcomes for all students. Chief among these for the purposes of this book is the School-to-Work Opportunities Act of 1994.

OVERVIEW OF SCHOOL-TO-WORK PROGRAMS

The School-to-Work Opportunities Act (STWOA) of 1994 (P.L. 103-239) provides a framework to help states and local communities develop comprehensive school-to-work transition programs (U.S. Department of Education,

1994). The overall purpose of school-to-work programs, as defined by the STWOA, is to prepare all students for work and further education, and increase their opportunities to enter first jobs in high-skill, high-wage careers. The STWOA defines all students to include both male and female students from a broad range of backgrounds and circumstances, including disadvantaged students, students from diverse racial, ethnic, or cultural backgrounds, students with disabilities, school dropouts, and academically talented students (Choy, Alt, & Henke, 1994; U.S. Department of Education, 1994). Congress recognized in the rationale for the Act that helping *all* students achieve better education and employment outcomes would require a fundamental restructuring of the educational delivery system, and greater coordination and collaboration among various categorical work-related education and training programs. Accordingly, the STWOA is intended to be part of a broader national initiative for comprehensive educational reform (e.g., the Goals 2000: Educate America Act of 1994), and school-to-work programs developed by states and local communities are intended to be part of a larger educational reform strategy undertaken by these entities as well (Kyle, 1995; Mendel, 1994). Similarly, the STWOA is intended to help states and local communities create a single, seamless, comprehensive school-to-work system that will replace the often fractured and fragmented education and job training programs that now exist under a variety of authorities and jurisdictions (Choy, 1994; Moore & Waldman, 1994).

It is helpful to view the school-to-work transition movement as an umbrella concept. No single school-to-work "model" is prescribed in the authorizing legislation (P.L. 103-239) nor in the emerging school-to-work literature. Rather, states and local communities are encouraged to use existing programs within education reform, worker preparation, and economic development efforts to build a school-to-work system that makes most sense for them. Although no model is prescribed, three components are considered basic to a comprehensive school-to-work program: school-based learning, work-based learning, and connecting activities. Together, these three components provide a framework to help local school-to-work programs accomplish the following goals: (a) encourage all students to stay in school and attain high standards of academic and occupational achievement; (b) make education more meaningful for all students by integrating academic and occupational learning, and providing this integrated instruction in applied settings in the community; and (c) enhance students' prospects for entry into work or further learning by building effective partnerships among secondary schools, postsecondary education institutions, employers, community agencies, parents, and students (U.S. Department of Education, 1994; U.S. Department of Labor, 1992).

School-based Learning Component

The school-based learning component of the STWOA calls for the provision of instructional programs and career guidance and planning services that expose students to a variety of career possibilities, help them select a career major based on their interests and abilities, and help them attain high standards of academic and occupational competence (U.S. Department of Education, 1994). The school-based learning component lies at the core of the educational restructuring called for by the STWOA, and is fundamental to increasing the likelihood that school-to-work programs will produce the structural changes in schools and educational outcomes for students that are envisioned by the Act (Grubb, 1994; Hamilton & Hamilton, 1994; Pauly, Kopp, & Haimson, 1994).

Central to the school-based learning component is the concept of a career major. Career majors provide a structure to integrate academic and occupational content and organize students' course work around broad career areas. They also provide purpose and direction for students' school experiences and result in the award of a high school diploma (or its equivalent) that has more relevance for students' postschool goals (Hamilton & Hamilton, 1994; U.S. Department of Education, 1994). The STWOA calls for students to make an initial selection of a career major no later than the 11th grade, but nothing in the language of the Act prevents this planning and selection process from beginning earlier in a student's school career. And, indeed, it should begin much earlier for students with disabilities (National Transition Network, 1994; Norman & Bourexis, 1995).

The STWOA identifies three additional elements of the school-based learning component that together provide a process for enhancing the selection and completion of a meaningful career major: (a) provision of career awareness, exploration, and counseling programs beginning no later than the 7th grade to help students make more informed educational and occupational choices; (b) regularly scheduled evaluations to help students assess their academic and occupational strengths, weaknesses, and progress; and (c) transition planning procedures to help students gain access to additional training or postsecondary educational opportunities (U.S. Department of Education, 1994). These elements are consistent with special education law and best practices for students with disabilities, and the STWOA recognizes that students with disabilities and certain other groups (e.g., young women, students of color) may need additional support services to benefit from these elements (National Transition Network, 1994; Norman & Bourexis, 1995).

Recent research documents the importance of these school-based elements for helping students with and without disabilities obtain better postschool outcomes. Rogers, Hubbard, Charner, Fraser, and Horne (1995) found in their evaluation of exemplary school-to-work programs nationwide that student outcomes were enhanced when programs organized school-based learning opportunities around career concepts, integrated career information and guidance activities into learning experiences, and created a progressive career exploration system that began in middle or elementary grades and continued throughout high school. Student success was also enhanced when programs provided students with options and support to access postsecondary education, and when the entire school-based learning component was structured to promote student self-determination, especially for students with special needs (e.g., at-risk students, students with disabilities). Benz, Yovanoff, and Doren (1997) examined school-to-work components that predicted better employment and educational outcomes one year out of school for students with and without disabilities. They found that students who possessed several of the career awareness, academic, and occupational skills targeted by the school-based learning component of school-to-work programs, and students who had their ongoing instructional needs addressed through postprogram planning activities, were substantially more likely to experience better employment and postsecondary educational outcomes. These relationships held true for both students with and without disabilities.

Work-based Learning Component

The work-based learning component of the STWOA emphasizes the importance of work and community environments as the context within which students learn to apply the academic and occupational knowledge and skills they acquire in their school-based learning opportunities. Work-based opportunities also provide students with "real-world" experiences to learn general workplace competencies (e.g., positive work habits, job-related social and communication skills) and occupational knowledge and skills related to the "industry sector" the student is planning to enter (U.S.

Department of Education, 1994). Providing students with these learning opportunities will require the active participation of employers, and the creation of multiple options, including: community service, field trips and job shadowing experiences, structured work experiences (including paid work experience), cooperative education programs, business–education compacts, school-based enterprises, youth apprenticeships, and job training (Goldberger, Kazis, & O'Flanagan, 1994; Hamilton & Hamilton, 1994). The establishment of workplace mentors who instruct students on-site in targeted knowledge and skills, in consultation with classroom teachers, is an essential element of the work-based learning component (Freedman & Baker, 1995).

Work-based learning opportunities must be structured and tied closely to school-based learning opportunities if they are to have real educational value, contribute to the attainment of high academic and occupational standards, and avoid becoming another disconnected "work experience" program (Grubb, 1994; Hamilton & Hamilton, 1994). Recent research has identified several features of effective work-based programs that increase the likelihood these programs will be tied to students' school-based experiences and contribute to a more meaningful educational experience for all students, including students with disabilities. First, work-based programs must include multiple learning opportunities that build on local market conditions and that are responsive to differences in students' interests, abilities, previous work histories, and future plans (Benz et al., 1997; Hamilton & Hamilton, 1994; Rogers et al., 1995). Second, an administrative structure must be established to manage the work-based component, including: (a) establishing program goals that all partners can agree upon, (b) providing training and ongoing support to work-site and school staff, (c) coordinating implementation of the program and communication between schools and work-sites, and (d) evaluating and documenting the progress individual students make in their placements and the overall program makes relative to its goals (Bailey & Merritt, 1993; Goldberger et al., 1994; McNeil & Kulick, 1995; Pauly et al., 1994; U.S. General Accounting Office, 1991). Finally, mechanisms must be established that provide students with orientation and initial training prior to participation in a work-site (e.g., interviewing skills, job-related social skills) and ongoing support and counseling during participation (e.g., help in resolving problems at work, help to cope with major personal and family crises) (Goldberger et al., 1994; Rogers et al., 1995).

Connecting Activities

This last component of school-to-work programs acknowledges that the worlds of school and work are largely alien to each other, and that connecting schools and workplaces does not happen naturally. The STWOA identifies several activities as important for connecting school-based and work-based learning components and secondary and postsecondary educational programs. Underlying all of these activities is the need to build effective partnerships among secondary schools, postsecondary education institutions, employers, and community agencies to ensure that students do not become the only "thread" that connects schools with these other partners (U.S. Department of Education, 1994; Weinbaum & Rogers, 1995).

The connecting activities identified in the STWOA include activities that focus on providing support to individual students and activities that encourage effective relationships between school-to-work programs and other partners. Connecting activities focused on providing support to individual students include (a) establishing school-site mentors to act as liaisons among students, employers, school staff, parents, and other appropriate community partners; (b) matching students with work-based learning opportunities; and (c) providing students with postprogram assistance to secure employment or continue their education/training, and link them with other community services that may be necessary to assure a successful transition from school to work (U.S. Department of Education, 1994; Weinbaum & Rogers, 1995).

Additional connecting activities focus on the administrative efforts necessary to build and maintain effective relationships between school-to-work programs and other community partners. These activities include (a) encouraging and supporting the active participation of employers and other community partners in the establishment and implementation of school-to-work efforts; (b) providing training and ongoing technical assistance to participating staff (e.g., teachers, employers, workplace mentors, school-site mentors, counselors) as they design and implement school-based and work-based learning components; (c) linking school-to-work efforts for youth with industry strategies for upgrading the skills of their workers; and (d) collecting information on postprogram outcomes of participants and using such information to evaluate the effectiveness of the program, including the program's effectiveness in serving students who historically have not been served well by public schools such as school dropouts, students of color, and students with disabilities (Orr, 1995; U.S. Department of Education, 1994; Weinbaum & Rogers, 1995).

There is strong support for the position taken in the Act that school-to-work programs should include connecting activities for both students and programs. The establishment of school–family–community partnerships as a strategy for improving school programs and community resources is an essential component of school restructuring efforts for the general population of students and school leavers (Kyle, 1995). Research documents that this dual approach is especially important for students with disabilities and other special needs (Benz, Lindstrom, & Halpern, 1995; Heal, Copher, & Rusch, 1990; Johnson & Rusch, 1993; Liontos, 1992). This dual approach assures that two related, yet distinctly different, purposes for building partnerships between schools and community organizations will be addressed: (a) to secure the community resources needed to help *an individual student* accomplish the transition goals identified by him or her, and (b) to improve the capacity of schools and communities to deliver services and provide resources that enhance the transition of *all students*.

GUIDING PRINCIPLES FOR THIS BOOK

The research just reviewed suggests that the school-based, work-based, and connecting activities components as defined in school-to-work legislation and literature have much to offer as a framework for building collaborative school-to-work programs for all students, including students with special needs. We will use this general framework across the remaining chapters of the book. Chapter 2, "Designing Instructional Options to Support Students' Transition Goals," includes ideas and strategies for helping students identify and prioritize the career/transition goals they believe are important and that should structure the services they receive in your program. This chapter also includes several strategies for designing school and community-based instructional options to help students learn the skills they have identified as important for their future. Chapter 3, "Creating Employment Opportunities for Youth," includes ideas and strategies for creating, implementing, and evaluating a variety of work-based learning opportunities for students. Chapter 4, "Providing Youth with Postprogram Placement and Follow-up Services," and Chapter 5, "Managing Collaborative School-to-Work Programs," address the connecting activities that are essential to ensuring student success in postschool environments.

Within this general framework, three principles guide the specific ideas and strategies discussed in this book. We believe these principles should guide all school-to-work programs, but they are especially important for youth with special needs. These principles highlight the breadth and intensity of school-to-work services that must be available if youth with special needs are to succeed. The vignette below describes an actual day in the life of a teacher in one of the YTP sites in Oregon. We believe it illustrates the real, everyday experiences of staff who are providing school-to-work services for youth with special needs, and provides a context for the importance of the principles that follow.

. . . .

A Day in the Life of a Special Needs School-to-Work Teacher

It's a rainy February morning. Tom Morelli has just finished his first cup of coffee and is reviewing his schedule for the day. "The first thing I need to do is give Jason a wake-up call. I promised I'd remind him about our appointment this morning." He makes the phone call from a wooden desk in the tiny corner bedroom, then walks out into the living room of the comfortable old house that is the hub of operations for the Centerville transition program.

Tom sits on the couch and reviews paperwork for a few minutes, then answers Jason's knock at the door. Jason has an appointment to talk with Tom about a new school-to-work program for adjudicated and emotionally disturbed youth. This is not their first meeting. About six weeks ago Jason was referred to the Centerville program by his case manager from the county. At that time he was homeless, bouncing back and forth between friends' houses and the local shelter while struggling to control his chronic mental illness. The first thing Tom did was help Jason move into a nearby apartment with a roommate. He explains, "Even though our program has a clear vocational emphasis, we couldn't really start there with Jason. He had too many other issues going on in his life. Some of my first questions with Jason were 'Do you have rent for January? How about electricity? Do you know where to go to get food?' Once those basic needs were satisfied, we could start talking about jobs."

Today's appointment is to complete the required intake paperwork to officially begin the program. Jason, a sturdy young man in dark blue jeans and work boots, sits in the armchair across from Tom and answers questions about his family and his personal history. Although he was enrolled in a special education program, Jason dropped out of high school several years ago. He once tried to take classes for high school completion at the local community college but "got lost out there" and never went back. Midway through the interview, he rubs his eyes and complains that he is feeling sore and tired today. With a hint of pride in his voice, he tells Tom that he worked all day yesterday unloading trucks. Unfortunately, the job is only temporary and he is still worried that he may lose his apartment. He also admits that the apartment is "getting crowded" with all of his roommate's friends hanging around, and that people are "always doing drugs there."

After signing the program intake forms, Tom and Jason agree to schedule a planning meeting early next week. The meeting will focus on Jason's short-term living needs, but Tom wants to also "take a look at your future—so it's important that all the right people are there." Jason decides to invite his roommate, his brother, his mother, and his vocational rehabilitation counselor. He carefully writes the date and time in his new appointment book. When Tom asks him what his schedule is for the rest of the day, he replies that he is headed to the blood bank to donate plasma. Then he will go over to the temp agency to turn in his time card and see if they have any more work for him. "Remember to call me to check in on Friday" Tom calls out. But Jason is already headed off into the rain to catch the bus.

Tom begins pulling information together for his next appointment, when the phone rings. It is a local university student who is completing a master's degree in education. She is hoping to get some college credit for volunteering in the Centerville program. Tom makes an appointment to see her, then returns to the living room to chat with Stacy, another student in the program. Stacy has dropped by because she wants to use the computer, and she really needs to talk with Tom about a blow-up she had last week. Tom takes 10 minutes to listen to Stacy. He reassures her with a promise to talk again soon, and agrees to let her work on some flyers on the computer while he finishes his next interview.

A few minutes later Lamont and Derek come in the door. Lamont is an intense young man who was just released from a juvenile corrections center for assaulting another student. Derek, his advocate, has been assigned to help Lamont get his life back on track now that he is living in the community again. Tom invites them to sit down, and begins describing the purpose of the program. "What we do is work one-on-one with you to find a job, and help you get any other services you need. We'll stay connected to you, but you also have to make a commitment to set some goals for yourself and follow through on your appointments with us." Lamont seems interested, and says that he really wants to move out into an apartment here in Centerville. He hopes to get a carpentry or construction job to support himself. Handing him an application form, Tom encourages Lamont to call next week to set up an initial appointment.

It's almost lunchtime now, and Tom needs to go across town to teach a class at Linfield Community College. On his way out the door he answers a phone call from Carlotta, another staff member. She wants Tom to measure the backyard garden space so she can give this information to the high school horticulture teacher for a meeting later today. Tom dashes outside with a string and tape measure, then relays the information to Carlotta. He grabs his cardboard box full of student workbooks and drives over to the college. The rain pours down steadily as he walks across the campus to the industrial education building. After checking in with the receptionist about the enrollment figures for this week, he sets up his teaching materials in the small second floor classroom. He takes a few minutes for a cup of coffee and a half sandwich at the college cafeteria before going upstairs to teach a "transition class" for high school completion students.

The class is new this year, part of the program's effort to coordinate services with the local community college. The students laugh and talk as they crowd into the 15 desks that fill the room. Most of them are here as part of an alternative program to earn credits for a high school diploma. Some are enrolled in basic education or vocational classes at the college. They settle down quickly as Tom begins to write on the board. "Today we're going to review the components of transition planning. Who can tell me one of the six areas of transition we talked about last time?" After a brief review, Tom leads them in a discussion about education, jobs, and living independently. Shawna, who at 15 already has a child of her own, comments that she is going to have to find a job soon to support herself. Many of the others want to work too, but they are unsure how to begin. Nathan wants a job that "is fun and makes a lot of money." After a 20-minute discussion about the realities of minimum wage jobs and the costs of apartments, Tom wraps up the class by saying. "This is what transition is all about—helping you think about how you want your life to be and how you will get there."

After class several students linger at the front of the room to talk with Tom. One young woman eagerly tells him about an opportunity she has to enroll in a medical technician program. Another student, who was strangely quiet during class, reveals that his father has kicked him out of the house. He has only 2 weeks to find a place to live and a job to support himself. Tom introduces him to one of the older community college students and sends them across campus to look at the job posting board. The classroom is empty now, and Tom has a few minutes to talk with Nancy, his assistant teacher, about next week. They make plans to co-teach next Tuesday's lesson, agreeing to meet again this evening for the parent orientation meeting.

On the way back to the transition house, Tom stops at the grocery store to buy snacks for the parent meeting. The rest of the staff are waiting for him in the living room, and they spend the next hour talking about plans for the garden project. Their idea is to use the garden beds behind the house as a job training site, and potentially a student-run business. The team is very excited about the possibility of putting together a program that will offer students the opportunity to learn horticulture, business, and marketing skills in a hands-on setting. When the staff meeting ends, Tom sets up for the last appointment of the day—a parent meeting for the students in the community college transition class. All of the parents were invited to come and talk about how they can support their students during the transition planning process. Although he sent a personal letter out to all of the parents, no one shows up for the meeting. He waits for 15 minutes, then clears off the big living room table. It's dark outside now, almost 7:00 p.m. He locks up the door, climbs into his blue pickup truck and heads for home.

. . . .

Keep the experiences of Tom Morelli and the needs of his students in mind as you review the following principles.

▶ *School-to-work programs for special needs youth must balance the importance of being part of school-to-work reform for all students with the need to provide the individualized instruction and support services required for special needs youth to succeed.*

The ideal approach articulated in school-to-work legislation and literature is to build a single, seamless school-to-work system that will meet the unique needs of all students, drawing from the many separate programs that now exist. In this approach there wouldn't be school-to-work programs for special needs youth. There would be *one* school-to-work system that meets the needs of *all* youth, including youth with special needs. This goal is a worthy one. School-to-work programs for special needs youth *must* be part of a comprehensive school-to-work reform effort that is intended to serve all students. Without a comprehensive effort focused on the *total* student population, school-to-work programs for youth with special needs will remain separate, vulnerable programs on the margins of "what schools really should be doing" (Benz & Kochhar, 1996; Grubb, 1994; Paris, 1994).

Yet, the reality in many local communities has caused some school-to-work proponents (e.g., Mendel, 1994) to question whether a single system could possibly meet the unique needs of all students. The goal of building a single, comprehensive school-to-work system in local communities must never occur at the expense of creating a meaningful array of services that address the school-to-work transition needs of students who require additional or greater support to succeed. The "one size fits all" approach may work in the marketing of clothing apparel, but it is no way to build a school-to-work program. School-to-work services and community partnerships should be determined by the specific needs of the students who are participating at any point in time, and must be responsive to the ways in which these needs change as students enter and exit over time.

Balancing these interests is critical to building stable, effective school-to-work programs that are central to the purposes and mission of schools. Planning approaches (e.g., Paris, 1994) have been proposed for developing school-to-work programs within the context of overall school change. These approaches, which typically include broad stakeholder participation and systematic planning activities, offer hope and guidance for creating school-to-work programs that are central to the mission of schools and responsive to the needs of students who historically have not been served well by the public schools. Ensuring that all youth have the individualized instruction and support services necessary to benefit from school-to-work programs will require administrative commitment, staff attitudes and expertise, and school and community resources beyond what have been available in schools traditionally (Lombard, Hazelkorn, & Miller, 1995). As we work toward this worthy goal of building an effective, responsive, comprehensive school-to-work system we must not lose sight of the immediate need to provide special needs youth with a more meaningful education and better outcomes.

▶ *School-to-work programs must help students address the full range of issues they will confront as they move from high school to adult life.*

The purpose of school-to-work programs, as defined in the Act, is to prepare all students for work and further education, and increase their opportunities to enter first jobs in high-skill, high-wage careers. There has been some concern expressed in the school-to-work literature that the phrase "school-to-work" is too limiting. Some authors argue that the term should be changed to "school-to-career" or "career opportunity system" (e.g., Hamilton & Hamilton, 1994). Still others have expressed concern that "life skills" content is missing from much of the discussion about school-to-work, and that *all* students need life skills instruction before they leave high school (Schultz, 1994).

School-to-work programs should help all students, especially special needs youth, address the full range of issues they will confront as they transition from school to adult life. Halpern (1994) has defined the transition process as "a change in status from behaving primarily as a student to assuming emergent adult roles in the community. These roles include employment, participating in post-secondary education, maintaining a home, becoming appropriately involved in the community, and experiencing satisfactory personal and social relationships" (p. 117). The Carnegie Commission on Adolescent Development (1995) arrived at similar conclusions about the desired outcomes of the school to community transition process.

> All adolescents must meet the same fundamental requirements if they are to be prepared for success in adulthood. They must find ways to earn respect, establish a sense of belonging to one or more highly valued groups, make close and enduring human relationships, and build a sense of personal worth based on useful skills. (p. 21)

These various quality of life dimensions (e.g., occupational, educational, personal–social) are often correlated with one another (Halpern, 1993), suggesting that program services cannot simply address one dimension of the transition process. Moreover, many of the personal, family, and educational obstacles experienced by youth with special needs tend to cluster in individuals and reinforce one another (Dryfoos, 1990). In our efforts to build better school-to-work programs, we must not lose sight of the other quality of life dimensions that so greatly impact the quality of worklife for transition-age youth—and for all of us.

> ▶ *School-to-work programs must foster student self-determination, and must include support services that recognize that dreaming and doubting go hand in hand for many youth, especially youth with special needs.*

School-to-work proponents increasingly advocate that student self-determination be a primary focus of the learning process, especially for at-risk students (Rogers et al., 1995). Fostering student self-determination as a goal of transition services has been advocated by best practices and promoted in special education and rehabilitation legislation for several years.

The importance of this approach is highlighted by years of research examining the outcomes experienced by young adults with disabilities. For example, Mithaug, Martin, Agran, and Rusch (1988), in their review of the extant follow-up research, noted:

> When do students with special needs fail? They fail because we no longer teach them, and they are on their own. . . . Students fail because they have not learned to be independent. They cannot adapt. And they do not know how to succeed. Students rarely experience independent success because schools rarely teach and support these skills. (p. 7–8)

The lesson is clear. No amount of community instruction, or special transition services, will insure that students will be successful *unless* they are also provided with opportunities and support to make their own decisions and direct their own futures.

At the same time, we know that acquiring self-determination skills, and learning to take responsibility for one's life, is not a straightforward, linear process for any young person. Consider the following quotes from Marion Wright Edelman and William Bennett.

> You are in charge of your own attitude. . . . Don't be afraid of failing. It's the way you learn to do things right. It doesn't matter how many times you fall down. What matters is how many times you get up. . . . Be a can-do, will-try person. Focus on what you have and not what you don't have, what you can do rather than what you cannot do. (Edelman, 1992, p. 71, 42, 65)

> Responsible persons are mature people who have taken charge of themselves and their conduct, who *own* their actions and *own up* to them— who *answer* for them. . . . How do we encourage our children to persevere, to persist in their efforts to improve themselves, their own lot, and the lot of others? By standing by them, and with them and behind them; by being coaches and cheerleaders, and by the witness of our own example. (Bennett, 1993, p. 186, 528)

School-to-work programs must support youth with special needs through the dreaming and doubting that accompanies the transition process. Helping youth dream about and plan for their future, and providing instructional opportunities to help them learn the skills and personal characteristics necessary to achieve their dreams is a daunting set of tasks for any program staff. Imagine for a moment how daunting it must feel for the young people who are experiencing it directly and personally. We must expect that dreaming and doubting will go hand in hand for many of the youth we work with. As one young woman in the YTP commented when asked what she hoped to accomplish in the program, "I want to work part-time and go to the community college to get my degree and maybe become a RN (registered nurse), but I don't know . . . maybe that probably won't work. . . . Most of my friends are just going to get a job, and I don't know how my mom or my boyfriend will take me going to school. . . . And sometimes I don't know if I can do it although I did get pretty good grades in school. I guess I'm really not sure." Helping students to become the "can-do, will-try" people that Marion Wright Edelman describes in the quote above will require that we design programs in which students and staff can serve as coaches, cheerleaders, and examples for one another.

There it is: a general school-to-work framework and three principles to guide your efforts. Your work on behalf of youth with special needs is very important. The task will be daunting at times, but no more so than the challenges facing the youth with whom you will be working. And the rewards that await you and the students you will be serving are worth the effort. We hope the ideas and strategies in this book will be useful as you build collaborative school-to-work programs for youth with special needs. Good luck.

CHAPTER 2

· ·

Designing Instructional Options To Support Students' Transition Goals

· ·

Where there is no vision, the people perish. Train up a child in the way he should go, and when he is old he will not depart from it.

(PROVERBS 29:18; 22:6, KING JAMES VERSION)

Adolescence is one of the most fascinating and complex transitions in the life span: a time of accelerated growth and change second only to infancy; a time of expanding horizons, self-discovery, and emerging independence. Many young people manage to negotiate their way through the critical adolescent years with relative ease. . . . For others, however, the obstacles in their path can impair their physical and emotional health, destroy their motivation and ability to succeed in school and jobs, and damage personal relationships. (Many of these) young people see into their future and find nothing to hope for. Others dream but often have no more than a vague image of the future as they embark on a prolonged search for the pathways to promising adulthood. . . . They must have the help of caring adults to develop a positive vision of the future, to see images of what adulthood offers and requires, and to prepare themselves for opportunities that are available to them. With appropriate guidance and support from families, schools, and other institutions, young people can grow up with the skills and values needed to participate in a humane, civil society.

(CARNEGIE COUNCIL ON ADOLESCENT DEVELOPMENT, 1995, P. 19, 21)

How do we help young people dream about their future, acquire knowledge and skills necessary for accomplishing (or revising) their dreams, and develop the work ethic and personal characteristics that are so central to leading fulfilling and productive lives? As the quotes above illustrate, questions such as these have been asked for thousands of years—and they remain at the forefront of our concerns for youth today.

Why is this relevant to a chapter on "Designing Instructional Options to Support Students' Transition Goals?" Helping students gain meaning and value from their educational experience is at the heart of the school-to-work reform movement. In Chapter 1 we briefly reviewed school-to-work legislation and literature, and concluded that the school-based component of school-to-work programs should include strategies to help students identify a general career path to guide the instruction and work experiences they receive through school-to-work programs. Further, the identification of a broad career path should take into consideration students' previous work histories and interests, and should be re-evaluated on a regular basis and modified if necessary. Finally, students should receive assistance to explore and connect with postsecondary options related to their career path. We also identified several principles that should guide school-to-work services for special needs youth, including ensuring that services address the full range of life issues confronting youth during the transition process, encouraging the development of student self-determination, and building school-to-work services in a manner to support the "ups and downs" that students inevitably experience during the school-to-community transition process.

The strategies in this chapter will help you develop and implement school-based instructional services using these principles. The chapter is divided into two major sections. In the first section, titled "Identifying and Prioritizing Transition Goals," strategies are described for surveying students' interests, preferences, and needs in order to determine the content and focus of instruction. The emphasis is on helping students identify what *they* believe is important to learn. The second section, titled "Developing New Instructional Options," describes several strategies for providing students with learning opportunities. These options have been developed and used in YTP sites across Oregon for the past several years. All of these options have been developed with the underlying philosophy of student self-determination and empowerment. This philosophy is manifested through the teaching of goal setting, problem solving, and self-advocacy skills, and by allowing students opportunities to dream and doubt—and experience failure and success—in a structured, supportive environment.

IDENTIFYING AND PRIORITIZING TRANSITION GOALS

Baseball great Yogi Berra has been quoted as saying "You got to be careful if you don't know where you are going, because you might not get there." The procedures described in this section of the chapter are intended to help students figure out where they want to go—to identify and prioritize their transition goals. They are organized into two basic steps: (a) help students identify their hopes and dreams for the future, and (b) help students develop a plan for instruction.

Little emphasis is placed on writing formal transition plans that will meet federal and state requirements governing transition planning for school (e.g., Individualized Education Plans) and community agencies (e.g., Individualized Written Rehabilitation Plans in Vocational Rehabilitation). Rather, emphasis is placed on providing students with the opportunity and support necessary to help them take greater ownership and responsibility for their future, and for identifying the instructional needs that must be addressed through your school-to-work program. The fundamental importance of this approach has been communicated to us strongly and consistently over the past several years through conversations with the students, parents, school, and adult agency staff we have worked with in communities across Oregon. Before you begin reading the procedures in this section, take a moment to read the vignette by Jack Canfield titled "Follow Your Dream." It does a marvelous job of describing the importance of dreams in shaping students' futures, *and* the influence that educators have in this process.

. . . .

Follow Your Dream

I have a friend named Monty Roberts who owns a horse ranch in San Ysidro. He has let me use his house to put on fund-raising events to raise money for youth at risk programs.

The last time I was there he introduced me by saying, "I want to tell you why I let Jack use my house. It all goes back to a story about a young man who was the son of an itinerant horse trainer who would go from stable to stable, race track to race track, farm to farm and ranch to ranch, training horses. As a result, the boy's high school career was continually interrupted. When he was a senior, he was asked to write a paper about what he wanted to be and do when he grew up."

"That night he wrote a seven-page paper describing his goal of someday owning a horse ranch. He wrote about his dream in great detail and he even drew a diagram of a 200-acre ranch, showing the location of all the buildings, the stables and the track. Then he drew a detailed floor plan for a 4,000-square-foot house that would sit on the 200-acre dream ranch."

"He put a great deal of his heart into the project and the next day he handed it in to his teacher. Two days later he received his paper back. On the front page was a large red F with a note that read, See me after class."

"The boy with the dream went to see the teacher after class and asked, 'Why did I receive an F?'

"The teacher said, 'This is an unrealistic dream for a young boy like you. You have no money. You come from an itinerant family. You have no resources. Owning a horse ranch requires a lot of money. You have to buy the land. You have to pay for the original breeding stock and later you'll have to pay large stud fees. There's no way you could ever do it.' Then the teacher added, 'If you will rewrite this paper with a more realistic goal, I will reconsider your grade.'

"The boy went home and thought about it long and hard. He asked his father what he should do. His father said, 'Look, son, you have to make up your own mind on this. However, I think it is a very important decision for you.'

"Finally, after sitting with it for a week, the boy turned in the same paper, making no changes at all. He stated, 'You can keep the F and I'll keep my dream.'

Monty then turned to the assembled group and said, "I tell you this story because you are sitting in my 4,000-square-foot house in the middle of my 200-acre horse ranch. I still have that school paper framed over the fireplace." He added, "The best part of the story is that two summers ago that same schoolteacher brought 30 kids to camp out on my ranch for a week." When the teacher was leaving, he said, 'Look, Monty, I can tell you this now. When I was your teacher, I was something of a dream stealer. During those years I stole a lot of kids' dreams. Fortunately you had enough gumption not to give up on yours.'

Don't let anyone steal your dreams. Follow your heart, no matter what. (Canfield, 1993, pp. 207–208)

. . . .

Help Students Identify Their Hopes and Dreams for the Future

Help students identify their interests and abilities

The first activity in helping students identify their hopes and dreams for the future is to help them think about their interests and abilities in different life areas related to being an adult (e.g., work, continuing education, living in the community). Interests and abilities are separate but related concepts. Usually, people are interested in things they are good at, and vice versa. Of course, this is not always true. Sometimes we are interested in doing something that we don't already know how to do, or know how to do very well. Consider, for example, the simultaneous increase in computer purchases by adults who never grew up with electronic video games, and the publication of numerous manuals on computers all of which end with the phrase ". . . for dummies."

Despite the fact that interests and abilities are different conceptually, many of the strategies for helping students identify their interests and abilities are similar, and discussions of interests and abilities often occur together naturally. For example, two equally appropriate ways to help students think about their interests and abilities might be to (a) first discuss interests across several life areas and then at a later time discuss abilities across those same life areas, or (b) discuss interests and abilities at the same time for one particular life area (e.g., school) and then discuss subsequent life areas at a later time. Regardless of the approach used, the end goal is the same, that students understand and are able to relate orally or in writing what their interests *and* abilities are across different life areas that are important to them.

At first, many students may be unable to tell you their "interests" or "abilities," either because they aren't often asked this by professional educators, or because they don't think about these issues using such terms. Don't let this deter you. Helping students understand their interests and abilities is fundamental to thinking about hopes and dreams for the future. There are a number of strategies to help students identify their interests and abilities, which generally can be grouped as formal and informal.

Although numerous formal instruments are available commercially to help students identify their interests and abilities, most are focused on occupations and career planning concepts. In this context, we are using *formal* to mean instruments that have been developed and tested using traditional test development procedures that allow for standardized scores and profiles to be produced on individuals. Comparisons are then made against scores and profiles for the larger group of persons on whom the test was standardized. Typically, the instruments that assess interests contain items that reflect actual job tasks performed in various occupations. Individuals are asked to indicate how much they like doing each item, usually using some kind of scale that includes descriptors such as "not very much" to "very much." Other variations of formal interest inventories ask individuals to indicate, typically through forced choice responses, which personal values they prefer in the activities or jobs they perform. Instruments that assess abilities typically require individuals to perform actual or paper and pencil activities that tap skills associated with different occupations. Other variations of ability instruments ask respondents to identify skills they have used in the past in different contexts and then to indicate how much they liked using each skill, again usually using some kind of scale that includes descriptors such as "not very much" to "very much." While formal instruments can be useful in helping students identify interests and abilities, by design they assume that individuals have had sufficient prior exposure to different activities or jobs and that they have already given some thought to different career possibilities based on these experiences. These may not be safe assumptions for many students with special needs.

Information on students' interests and abilities can also be solicited through more informal strategies. This approach has been used most often in YTP sites in Oregon and, generally, YTP personnel have used a three-step process to help students begin thinking about their interests and abilities: (a) gather available information on students, and help them to organize and review this information; (b) meet with students individually or in small groups to discuss interests and abilities; and (c) conduct a more structured, intensive process (e.g., person-centered planning approaches) for students who needed the additional support to identify interests and abilities.

First, gather available information on students, including for example: (a) school records, (b) anecdotal or observational information from school staff and parents, (c) screening information collected as the student was entering your program (this is discussed in more detail in Chapter 5), and (d) current/previous IEPs (Individualized Education Plans) for students who are or were receiving special education services. Help students to organize and review this information for indications of interests and abilities. Before meeting with the student, you may want to review this information carefully yourself to think about how this information could be useful. While previous school-related records can be helpful under certain circumstances, frankly, our experience is that they too often identify tasks students can't do or aren't doing right. The purpose here is not to deny that these issues and needs exist, but rather to focus on what students want and can do. Many of the students you will be working with have heard the negative aspects repeatedly throughout their school careers. There will be plenty of time to incorporate these realities into their plans later. Stay focused on the positive at this point.

Second, meet with students individually or in small groups to begin discussions about their interests and abilities. These should be informal conversations directed at helping you discover the dreams, interests, and abilities of your students, and helping them uncover this in themselves. For example, students can be asked to think about and describe what things they like and dislike, what things they are good at and not good at. This is a strategy used commonly across many career and life planning curricula that have been published in the past few years. It is sometimes easier for students to identify likes and dislikes if they think about them in specific life areas such as school, leisure, friends, home, and work. Sometimes students have difficulty generating ideas because they tend to think of experiences in their entirety, "There is nothing about school that I like!" In these situations it is sometimes useful to help students look at *parts* of activities (e.g., a particular class in school or even particular aspects of a class; specific components of a job or volunteer activity in the community). A form you and your students can use to record their interests and abilities is provided in Appendix 2.1.

Many students will be able to identify interests and abilities on their own, together with a program staff person, or in small groups of students with a program staff person acting as a facilitator. Some students, however, will need a more structured process to help them generate ideas about their interests and abilities. For these students consider other strategies—such as "person-centered" planning approaches—that more systematically incorporate the ideas of other key people who are involved in the student's life such as family members, relatives, friends, teachers, or adult agency staff working with the student (e.g., a vocational rehabilitation counselor). YTP staff in Oregon who have used person-centered planning approaches with students have concluded that, even though they are more labor and time intensive than the approaches described above, they can be a very affirming experience for a student who is "stuck" and unable to generate ideas about interests and abilities. When done well, these approaches also lend themselves naturally to the kinds of goal setting activities discussed next.

One final set of comments about helping students identify their interests and abilities: A number of resources are available commercially to help students think about their interests, values, strengths, and abilities. YTP sites in Oregon have taken an eclectic approach to helping students identify their interests and abilities, drawing upon and combining a number of resources and strategies. We encourage you to do the same. No one tool will be sufficient for every student. In your pursuit to help students identify their interests and abilities, don't be afraid to demonstrate the qualities and characteristics that you ultimately want to see your students demonstrate. Be creative, resourceful, bold, patient, and persistent. The rewards to be gained by you and your students in terms of new insights about their interests and abilities are well worth the effort.

Help students identify goals in areas that are important to them

Thinking about the future and developing long- and short-term goals to get there are not skills that come naturally or easily to most young people. Nevertheless, they are fundamental to beginning the process of turning hopes and dreams into reality, and they are skills that young people *can* learn. Many of your students may find it difficult to set concrete, measurable goals at this point in the process. That's okay. Your task and theirs at this point is to identify one or more general goals that will begin to translate their interests and abilities into a vision of their future. Students sometimes have difficulty thinking about the future for the same reason they have difficulty thinking concretely about their interests and abilities—they tend to view experiences in their entirety. To the extent this is true, it can make the future a vague and overwhelming concept.

One strategy for helping students with initial goal setting is to help them think about specific aspects of the future, and then to think about one or more general goals in each of these areas. YTP sites in Oregon have used the graphic in Appendix 2.2 as a discussion starter with students. A Goal Summary Sheet is also included. Typically, staff have encouraged students to think about general goals related to work, continuing education, and living in the community. The areas identified on the graphic—where to live, transportation, friendships, leisure options, health needs, and civic responsibility—are all possible dimensions of living in the community, and they simply help students think about whether any of these different aspects of life in the community are relevant to them at this point in time.

Many of the instructional options discussed later in this chapter, such as Job Club, specifically target the development of goal setting as part of the program. Our experience in sites across Oregon is that special needs students will acquire the ability to set and accomplish their goals—and to own and take responsibility for them—if you build these learning opportunities into your program. Frankly, one of the biggest challenges we face in this effort is our own attitudes as adults about what is "realistic" for our students.

Earlier we presented a story by Jack Canfield titled "Follow Your Dream" that describes the lessons one particular teacher learned about supporting the dreams of his at-risk students. We've learned similar lessons over the past several years building school-to-work programs for special needs students. Our experience with Jared (a pseudonym) is presented next. As you read this vignette, think about what it really means to give students opportunities to take control over their lives.

. . . .

Jared's Story

Jared is a tall, energetic young man who likes to talk and joke. He grew up living with his mother. She was divorced from Jared's father, remarried, and has been separated from Jared's stepfather for several years. Jared's disabilities were not diagnosed until he reached adolescence. In middle school, he started showing serious behavior problems—conflicts with peers outside of his classes, impulsive acting-out, temper outbursts, non-compliance with teachers and other authority figures in the school, and truancy and fighting. When Jared was in 7th grade, he was diagnosed with Attention Deficit Disorder and Behavior Conduct Disorder and became eligible for special education services. He was placed in a self-contained classroom for Seriously Emotionally Disturbed (SED) students, taking 2 of his 8 classes in the mainstream.

When Jared entered high school, his participation in mainstream classes increased to 80 percent of his course schedule. In 10th grade, Jared requested that his connection with the SED program be severed. Jared's mother supported his desire to be removed from the SED program. But she expressed the hope that "there was some way that Jared's behavior could be monitored even if he was no longer in the program." She felt that even though he still had a number of problem areas, "this was part of the process of growing up and that it was necessary to let Jared start making certain decisions for himself." The teachers and staff agreed to remove Jared from the SED program his junior year, with some monitoring from his SED teacher and the provision he would be pulled back into the program if he failed two or more classes at any time during the school year. The next year, however, Jared's non-compliant behavior increased to such a degree that his SED teacher encouraged Jared to drop-out of high school and enroll in the community college's high school completion program. Jared's mother and the community college staff supported this decision. Jared followed through with this plan but, being exposed to older kids in a large, unfamiliar environment,

Jared "fell in with the wrong crowd" and started abusing alcohol. That spring, Jared was admitted to an adolescent alcohol and drug treatment center.

Jared's case manager at the treatment center knew of the YTP program. He contacted the YTP Teacher Coordinator regarding Jared's after-care needs for guidance and support. At that time, Jared was 16 years old. The Teacher Coordinator agreed to work with Jared and began the application process for YTP. At entry into the YTP, Jared stated that his career goal was to join the military. Notes in Jared's case files indicate that the professionals working with Jared at that time—YTP staff, treatment center staff, and Jared's Vocational Rehabilitation (VR) Counselor—all felt the military "was an unrealistic avenue for him to pursue." Nevertheless, this remained as a possible option to be explored. YTP staff and the VR Counselor helped Jared develop a transition plan that included employment, continuing education, job-training, help obtaining his driver's license, and ongoing counseling.

His Transition Specialist became someone whom, his mother said, Jared "looked up to and trusted very much." She developed and provided on-the-job training and intervention support for Jared over the duration of his time in the program. His Transition Specialist also spent considerable time talking through issues with Jared and giving him "lots of space." Through these interactions, she helped him understand better the "cause and effect nature" of his interactions with other people. She helped Jared develop a Behavioral Assessment Checklist that he could use to rate his own behavior on a daily basis. During this time, Jared was also continuing his substance abuse after-care. By the end of Jared's different job training placements, his Transition Specialist felt "Jared (had) improved in his attitude and interactions with co-workers. He accepts occasional teasing well and has learned to laugh at himself. In an incident occurring when a co-worker/assistant supervisor approached Jared in a challenging and intimidating manner, Jared showed diplomacy and self-control in this situation and took the appropriate steps to resolve the problem in a calm manner." Jared had been fired from a job earlier in high school because he reacted inappropriately to a similar situation.

As part of his transition plan, Jared enrolled in the community college's high school completion program. Completing his high school degree was a necessary step for Jared to become eligible to apply to the military. YTP staff felt that the community college, with support from program staff, was a better educational environment for Jared than his former high school. Six months after re-enrolling in the community college program, Jared became the first SED student from his school district to graduate successfully from the college's high school completion program. While Jared was attending classes at the college and working, he also passed the test to obtain his driving permit, successfully completed driving lessons, and secured his driver's license.

As Jared was nearing completion of his vocational and educational goals in YTP, he applied and was accepted into the U.S. Marines. In May of what would have been his senior year in high school, Jared started basic training. At first his transition into the Marines was lonely for him. His mother and the YTP staff all wrote Jared letters to encourage him and give him emotional support. Jared completed boot camp and attended advanced training in the Marine Corps. Since the time he finished advanced training, Jared has successfully completed a tour of duty in the Mediterranean, was stationed at a military base on the East Coast, and recently was stationed at a Marine Corps facility on the West Coast. A year ago Jared married, and he and his wife are now expecting their first child. After his military obligation is completed, Jared is planning a career as a firefighter.

. . . .

Jared had a dream of entering the military when he came into the program in this local YTP site. Yet, his background and profile at that time made it highly unlikely that he would ever achieve his dream, and the school and VR staff who were going to work with Jared through the program were quite justified in their belief that becoming a Marine would be an unrealistic goal for Jared. Fortunately for Jared these staff kept their skepticism in check, and instead helped him to focus on the things he would need to do to achieve his dream. The importance and power of owning his dream helped Jared accomplish what he needed to do, and when he entered—and eventually served successfully—in the military it was a proud moment for Jared, his family, and the program staff.

Some students will have clear ideas about their future, and other students will need considerable support to begin thinking about their future and identifying even general goals that would structure their participation in your program. The goals they set now will be refined and revised as they move further along in your program. That is the nature of the relationship between goals and experiences for all of us. We've all heard about (and may even have worked with) the stereotypic student who wants to be a rocket scientist or a rock star. We have a dual obligation to honor and respect our students hopes and dreams for the future, and to provide the learning opportunities and support services necessary to help them understand the evolving nature of dreams, goals, and experiences.

Help Students Develop a Plan for Instruction

Help students identify their instructional needs and priorities

Once students have a general idea of their interests and abilities, and of the goals that relate to their future hopes and dreams, they are in a better position to take responsibility for identifying their instructional needs and priorities. As before, this may be daunting for some students. Most young adults are not accustomed to having professionals seek their input in program design. Perhaps we fear that allowing students to identify their instructional needs and priorities could lead to the end result proposed by the irrepressible Calvin in the cartoon below.

The first step in helping students identify their instructional needs and priorities is to help them self-assess their current skill levels. Again, this could be a new and difficult task for many students. It isn't consistent with their previous experiences. Assessment in schools typically is something that is done *to, for,* and *on* students. Giving students the opportunity and responsibility to complete a careful self-assessment of their current skill levels is an essential component of helping students assume greater responsibility and ownership of the learning process.

As we described at the beginning of this chapter, it is important to gauge students' current level of performance in academic, independent living, personal/social, and vocational content areas—the four areas most commonly

Calvin and Hobbes   by Bill Watterson

associated with living and working successfully in the community. Some information on current skill levels will already have been gathered through the screening process as students enter your program, and through the process of helping students identify their interests and abilities. Throughout these earlier processes, you helped students focus on their strengths rather than their weaknesses. Now that they have a clearer sense of their interests and abilities and their hopes and goals for the future, students can and should be given the opportunity to identify their functional strengths *and* weaknesses in light of the initial decisions they have already made.

A number of functional skill checklists have been published over the past several years that you could use to help students identify their strengths and instructional needs in academic, vocational, independent living, and personal–social content areas. YTP sites in Oregon have used an instrument developed originally at the University of Oregon titled the Transition Skills Inventory. The Transition Skills Inventory has recently been updated, with versions created for students, parents, and teachers, and published as part of the *NEXT S.T.E.P.* (Halpern et al., 1997) curriculum to teach self-directed transition planning skills to students. The student version of the Transition Skills Inventory is included in Appendix 2.3. Typically, staff in YTP sites have worked with students individually or in small groups to help them complete the Transition Skills Inventory. Students are encouraged to seek the input of other key individuals (e.g., family, peers, teachers) to help in this self-assessment, especially for items about which they have doubts. It is not unusual for there to be some disagreement between students and parents or teachers regarding the student's current skill levels on some items. That's okay. You will want to help students understand that (a) everyone has things they do well and things they don't do well; (b) people can have different opinions about what those things are, and all opinions are valid; and (c) everyone can learn to do things better if they are motivated and willing to work hard at it.

Once students have completed their self-assessments, they are in a better position to identify their priorities for instruction. Students now have a sense of where they want to go (hopes, goals, interests) and from where they are starting (abilities, current skill levels). Your goal at this point is to help individual students identify their highest priorities for instruction, and in turn, help staff identify the highest instructional priorities for the program based on the collective needs and priorities of students. You can get input by meeting with students individually or in small groups. Small group meetings with students can be very energizing for staff and empowering for students as both begin to see students having real opportunities and responsibilities for creating the instructional priorities for the program. To make the most of these meetings students should review the written summaries of their goals, interests and abilities, and current skill levels, and attempt to answer questions such as: "What do I need to learn in order to work toward my goals?" or "What am I really interested in and excited about learning that will help me live and work in the community after I leave school?" Staff should also review these materials for all of the students who will be participating in the discussion session.

The Summary of Instructional Needs and Priorities form in Appendix 2.4 provides a format for structuring and summarizing these discussions. This form, which could also be replicated onto a chalkboard or large paper for all participants to see, provides a way to record instructional needs and preferences for individual students and for the groups of students. For each general area you might list some possible topics for instruction, and ask students to generate more. Or, you might let students brainstorm ideas, and then you can go back later and put them into the categories. The point is to find out the skills students think they already know, and the skills they *want and need* to learn to be more independent. Through this discussion process you should have a general list of topics that students believe are important to cover in any instruction provided. Your completed summary sheets should give you a picture of student preferences as well as specific needs for instruction. Look at the totals column, and make a list of the specific skill areas that have the highest totals. These are the highest priority needs for instruction as identified by students. You may also want to include on the summary sheet skills that students haven't identified but that you or your staff believe are priorities for instruction.

Help students develop, implement, and evaluate an instructional plan

At this point, you are ready to help students translate their decisions into a plan for instruction. This plan will shape how students use the resources of your school-to-work program, and other resources in the school and community, to achieve the transition goals they have established for themselves. As we mentioned earlier, we are not offering suggestions for writing transition plans in this book, nor are we providing sample plan forms for this purpose. There is such a diversity of plan documents in schools (e.g., Individualized Education Plans—IEPs) and community agencies (e.g., Individualized

Written Rehabilitation Plans—IWRPs) that anything we offered would be meaningless in most local communities. Moveover, we want to encourage you to focus on the planning process rather than the plan document. The activities described above are intended to help you develop a structured process that allows students to take responsibility and ownership for their transition goals and instructional planning.

The importance of supporting students as they implement, evaluate, revise, and eventually complete their instructional programs cannot be overemphasized. Don't lose sight of the principle of helping students actualize their dreams and overcome their doubts. Local YTP sites in Oregon have developed a variety of administrative strategies for regularly evaluating individual students' progress, including holding regular staff meetings of key personnel to discuss the status of students, and developing student case files to document instructional goals identified and completed. These strategies are discussed in more detail in Chapter 5. Providing students with appropriate levels of support is fundamental to determining which combination of *instructional* options your program creates.

Identify instructional options for helping students meet their transition goals

There are three general options for providing instruction to meet students' transition goals: (a) enroll students in existing school or community programs that will appropriately meet their instructional needs, and use your staff to monitor their progress; (b) provide individualized instruction or 1:1 tutoring to students; and (c) develop a *new* program or instructional option for groups of students with similar needs. The advantages and disadvantages of each of these options are summarized in Table 2.1.

To determine which options are appropriate for your program, review the instructional summary sheets that emerged from your discussions with students to determine if the instructional priorities identified through this process translate easily into any logical groupings for instruction. For example, if many of your students want and need to learn how to drive, you may decide to develop a class to prepare them to get their driver's permits. Or, if many of your students need to learn how to develop resumes and interview for jobs, you might consider developing a job club. If you find that your students' needs are varied, you may have to address them by providing individualized instruction, or by connecting students to existing instructional resources in the school or community. As you can probably guess from these

Table 2.1
Summary of Instructional Design Options

Options	Examples	Advantages	Disadvantages
Accessing existing programs	✔ enrolling students in high school cooperative work experience programs	✔ integrates students into the mainstream of educational programs	✔ may not meet the individual instructional needs of all students
	✔ referring students to a federal job training program, such as Job Corps	✔ less effort spent on developing "special" programs	
Providing 1-to-1 tutoring or assistance	✔ working with individual students to prepare them for a specific job interview	✔ meets specific needs of individual students	✔ time consuming for staff
	✔ providing individual tutoring or other support to assist students in passing academic course work		
Developing a new program	✔ developing a transition class within the high school curriculum	✔ provides a structured format for delivering instruction	✔ can create isolated or "special" programs for at-risk populations
	✔ working in collaboration with VR to develop a "job club" for youth in transition	✔ creates an opportunity for peer networking and support	✔ takes initial investment of time and energy to develop new options

few examples, most YTP sites in Oregon have found it necessary to use all three of these options to fully meet their students' instructional needs.

Find out what resources exist within the school (e.g., cooperative work experience programs, professional technical education, career education, personal finance, and life skills classes) and the community (e.g., local, state, or federal job training programs, academic and occupational classes at a community college, community agencies providing services or resources) that could address the instructional needs you prioritized earlier. You may have already collected this information during the referral and planning process, or your school district may have developed a resource manual that includes this information. If you aren't already familiar with these resources, take time to visit these programs. Meet with the staff and ask questions. Try to match the resources available and the instructional and support needs of your students. If a mismatch exists, try to determine the extent to which these resource providers are interested in working with your program to better address the needs of the kinds of students you will be serving.

You will also want to consider the advantages and disadvantages of participating in these programs versus creating a program specifically for your students. On the one hand, developing new instructional options designed to meet the needs of your students can help to create long-term systems change within your district. However, you need to also be cautious about being seen as a "stand-alone" program. It is important that school-to-work programs for special needs students be integrated within school-to work programs being developed for *all* students. It is important to be seen as a team player, and a potential resource in building collaborative transition programs. If you choose to use existing programs, or to provide individualized instruction, you will need to develop a plan of action with your team and move ahead using those strategies. If you decide to develop a new program, the next section describes several instructional models for you to consider.

DEVELOPING NEW INSTRUCTIONAL OPTIONS

The preceding section described strategies for helping students identify and prioritize their instructional needs, and develop a plan for learning skills that are important to them. This section describes procedures for developing four different instructional program options that will help students acquire these skills: (a) mentorship programs, (b) job clubs, (c) individual transition classes built into secondary or postsecondary course offerings, and (d) independent living apartment programs. Table 2.2 summarizes the features and benefits of each model. The instructional models in this chapter were developed by local YTP staff to better prepare students for the transition from school-to-work. These staff members at various sites believed that students needed the opportunity to learn in new ways outside the four walls of the classroom. Many of these students had failed in the traditional academic environment where success depended on completing homework and performing well on tests. Yet when these same students were placed in a local business alongside a community mentor, or given the support to develop

Table 2.2
Overview of Instructional Models

Models	Content Areas Addressed	Possible Locations	Unique Features
Mentorship Program	**Vocational:** career exploration, job specific skills, work behaviors **Personal/Social:** critical thinking, decision making, effective communication, interaction with peers and adult role models	community business	✔ familiarize students with diverse employment opportunities ✔ provides field experience in the workplace ✔ helps direct students toward career and educational goals
Job Club	**Vocational:** job search skills, job keeping skills, career exploration and decision making **Personal/Social:** problem solving, goal setting, peer support, self-advocacy	Vocational Rehabilitation office community meeting room high school classroom or lounge	✔ Offers a peer support group for processing job-related and personal issues ✔ Focuses on goal setting and life planning
Transition Class	**Academics:** consumer math **Vocational:** career exploration, job search skills **Independent Living:** driver education, community access, money management **Personal/Social:** social skills for job success, goal setting, problem solving	high school community college	✔ Provides structured instruction on a wide variety of critical transition topics, including: employment, continuing education, and independent living
Independent Living Apartment Program	**Academics:** consumer math, banking and budgeting **Independent Living:** cooking and nutrition, housekeeping, shopping **Personal/Social:** peer interactions, decision making	house or apartment in the community	✔ Offers an opportunity to learn and practice independent living skills in a real world setting

career goals through a job club, learning suddenly started to make sense for them.

Mentorship Program

Ask successful people about what has made a difference in their lives. As often as not, the "what" will be a "who"—an adult who showed a special interest, or who inspired, guided, and challenged them during adolescence. A teacher or relative can sometimes fill this role, but such adult–youth mentoring relationships can also be pre-arranged and structured to help ensure success. In typical mentorship programs, youth (sometimes called interns) are matched with positive adult role models. The pairs meet on a regular basis, usually at the mentor's place of employment. This type of positive adult interaction can help motivate students, and inspire them to stay in school or pursue challenging careers. The experiences of one YTP site with creating and using a mentorship program to address the school-to-work instruction needs of students are described in the following vignette.

· ·

Blue Valley Mentor Program

The Blue Valley mentorship program all started with a simple desire— to help students find good jobs. A team of special education staff from the high school and a counselor from the local Vocational Rehabilitation office started by developing a program to assist students with disabilities to obtain paid community employment. After spending some time doing an initial assessment of the students' strengths and weaknesses, the newly hired transition specialist realized she couldn't just start by calling employers and putting her students to work. "How can I go out and represent these students to the business community?" she wondered. "They don't have some of the *basic skills* they need to enter the workforce."

Although these students were on track to complete high school, they hadn't had the opportunity to learn the vocational and social skills needed to be successful on the job. So the transition specialist, working with a group of advisers from the school and community, began to develop a new work-based learning option—the mentor program. The purpose of the mentor program was to give these students an opportunity to develop work skills and to instill a strong work ethic by providing a variety of experiences in the community.

During the first year of the mentor program, 12 students with disabilities were matched with 12 adult mentors from the business community. The mentors were from all walks of life, including the Blue Valley city manager, a golf course maintenance specialist, and a computer expert from a large resort hotel. Each pair met once a week in the mentor's place of business and completed a series of assignments, designed to help the students understand the demands of a specific occupation as well as their own strengths and career interests. Students watched, listened, and learned through hands-on experiences.

After that first year, many of the students went on to paid jobs either in their mentorship site, or in a related occupation. The program was so successful that staff at the high school decided that it should be expanded to serve additional students. Currently all seniors at the high school participate in the mentor program. Over 200 employers are involved, and the program has become the model for school-to-work services for the entire region. In the words of one mentor, "The true benefit of this program is the remarkable impact these experiences have on kids."

· ·

Your first activity to establish a mentorship program should be to develop a brief program description that outlines its general structure, including goals and the students it is designed to serve. This written overview will be helpful as you lobby to get support for the program within the school and community. The information-gathering suggestions we offered at the beginning of this section of the chapter will help you generate some initial ideas for this program description. Based on our experiences with local sites that participate in the YTP, we recommend 10 basic steps to develop a mentorship program:

1. obtain support for your concept within the school;

2. obtain support within the community;

3. develop materials needed for the program;

4. select the students who will be involved;

5. provide orientation and training for community mentors;

6. match students with community mentors;

7. arrange for the initial meeting;

8. provide classroom instruction/orientation;

9. provide support to students and mentors; and

10. monitor and evaluate the success of the program.

Obtain support within the school

Before you can move ahead with implementing the mentorship program you need to have school administrative support. Set up a meeting with school administrators to describe the proposed mentor program, and obtain their input and support for developing the program. Specific issues to discuss at this meeting include:

- Who will coordinate and manage the program?
- When will students actually meet with their mentors, and how will this fit into their regular daily schedules?
- What student skills will be emphasized in the program?
- Will the school offer credit for students who participate in the mentor program?
- How will students be chosen or screened for the mentor program?
- How will community mentors be screened and trained?
- How will students get to their mentor site?

Obtain support within the community

The next step is to identify individual community members who might be interested in serving as mentors. Start by brainstorming a list of possibilities. You might want to consider employers who have hired students in the past, members of service clubs or other business groups, employers in specific industries, friends, neighbors, or other prominent community members. After you have developed your list, contact these individuals to assess their interest in participating. Describe the purpose of the program, the time commitment involved, and the benefits to *both* students and mentors. Ask the mentors for an initial commitment to participate, and explain that you will contact them again when you have identified a specific student for them to mentor. A sample Mentor Program Fact Sheet is included in Appendix 2.5 to help you with this process.

Develop materials

Many local school districts have developed mentorship and internship curriculum materials, with learning activities for mentors and students to complete. Depending on your goals for this program, you may want to adapt the materials already developed or design new materials to meet the needs of your students. Whatever direction you choose, your materials should clearly spell out the roles and responsibilities of both the mentor and the student, the methods for evaluating mentoring outcomes, and strategies for both mentors and students to receive support and follow-up. A example of how one mentorship program documented these community mentor and student/intern responsibilities is included in Appendix 2.6.

Select students to participate

You may decide to have all of the students in a particular grade or class participate in the mentor program, or only certain individuals who have expressed an interest. In either case, it is helpful to have prospective students complete a program application, which includes a brief job history, employment goals, and general interest areas. To help you get started, a sample program application is included in Appendix 2.7. Review the completed applications, and for each student note areas of occupational interest and possible mentor sites.

Provide orientation and training for community mentors

Now that you have selected the students who will participate, it is time to get a firm commitment from your community mentors. Many programs provide information to mentors by hosting a group orientation meeting. This is a time to pass out written information on the program, provide opportunities to share information and answer questions, and help mentors and student participants meet other program participants. At the meeting you should describe the purpose of the mentor program and the roles, responsibilities, and time commitments of mentors and student participants during the life of the mentoring relationship. You should also discuss the kinds of issues that can arise between mentors and student participants, provide opportunities for questions, and describe strategies that can be used by mentors and student participants to discuss and resolve issues that may arise. Finally, provide mentors and students with information on how to contact program staff with questions once the mentoring relationship begins.

Match students with mentors

Students can be matched with mentors in several ways:

- Students can request a specific occupation, or even a specific person for their mentor.
- Students may request to be placed with several different mentors to explore different jobs, spending a limited amount of time with each one. (This is especially useful if students are unsure of their career goals.)
- School staff can select a mentor for the student based on the information gathered in the application process.

This initial matching process is a critical component of the entire mentoring process. Adults and students with similar interests and even similar temperaments have often created successful matches. Many of the most successful adult/student combinations have blossomed into long-term mentoring relationships.

Arrange for the initial meeting

Once you have matched each student with a prospective mentor, school staff should contact potential mentors who were identified in the initial start-up phase, and reconfirm their interest in participating. The next step is for the student to contact the mentor, and set up the initial meeting. During this meeting, students should be given a tour of the business, and a general explanation of the mentor's job duties. Both mentors and students should be encouraged to discuss with each other their goals and expectations for the time they will be spending together.

Some mentorship programs treat this initial meeting as a job interview, giving the community mentor an opportunity to ask the prospective intern questions, and the student an opportunity to find out more about the potential placement site. If desired, students can arrange to interview at several mentor sites. When both parties are satisfied that a good match has been made, then the actual mentoring activities can begin.

Provide classroom instruction

Many mentorship programs include a school-based component. Class meetings are scheduled either for the first few weeks *before* students begin their work placement or at regular intervals *during* the mentoring experience. The first class session should give students an orientation to the goals and expectations of the mentoring program. During subsequent sessions, students can be introduced to various career options through guest speakers or class discussions. Students may also complete written assignments describing the requirements of certain occupations. Regular class meetings are also an important time for students to "check-in" with the school staff and discuss any issues or concerns.

Provide support to mentors and students

After the mentorship placements have been established, it is important for school staff to help monitor the activities occurring at the job site. Some mentorship programs use workbooks with required lessons to complete, others ask students to write about their experiences in a journal on a daily basis. Time sheets are also useful to document the number of hours students spent at the community workplace.

Staff must provide support and structure to the mentors. Use the suggestions for community mentors included in Appendix 2.8 as a way to help mentors understand the type of information they should provide students in their regular meetings. It will also be important to contact mentors on a regular basis to check on student progress. Find out if the student is having any difficulties—either in keeping to the established schedule or in completing the tasks the mentor has assigned. Is the mentor satisfied that the student is making progress in meeting his/her goals? In some cases, students may need to be matched with a different mentor if problems don't seem easily resolved. Both mentors and students need to know there are established and constructive ways to alter or end their relationship. Remember that mentoring relationships are a "two-way street" that require both parties to actively participate, communicate, and problem solve in order to have a meaningful and successful experience.

At the completion of a mentorship placement, school staff should schedule a final meeting with each student/mentor pair. This is a time for the students and mentors to discuss their experience and talk about what they have learned. School staff should also review any written assignments students have completed, and, if this has been negotiated in advance, award school credit.

Evaluate the success of the program

The final step in developing any new program is to evaluate its impact. Program staff should gather evaluation information from mentors and students to determine the overall effectiveness of the mentorship program. Consider using a business-driven evaluation tool such as a consumer satisfaction survey to collect information from the mentors. Students should have the opportunity to evaluate their experience as well. Based on this feedback, school and business representatives should meet to determine how the program could be improved, and ultimately whether to maintain the mentor program as an instructional option for students in transition from school to work.

Job Club

Job clubs are support groups for people who are searching for jobs. In a typical job club, members meet on a regular basis to update resumes, practice job interviewing skills, and serve as support to each other during the job search process. Once a job club member is successfully employed, he/she no longer attends the group. Over the past several years, many YTP sites in Oregon have taken this traditional job club model and adapted it to meet the needs of students in transition. These school-based job clubs teach job search skills in an informal environment, and provide a safe place for students to discuss hopes and dreams for the future. Job clubs for students in transition have included special education students between the ages of 16 and 21 who are either looking for work or who are already working in the community. Job club members may be currently enrolled high school students, school drop-outs, or high school graduates who need additional support to meet their transition goals. The experiences of one YTP site with creating and using a job club to address the school-to-work instruction needs of students are described in the following vignette.

· ·

Springdale Job Club

Walk into the Brattain House, across the street from Springdale High School, at 4 p.m. on any Thursday and you will see a group of young people sitting comfortably around a big table. The students are snacking on chips and soda pop, and talking intently about their hopes and dreams for the future. "My long-term goal is be the head coach of a girl's basketball team," one young woman shares with the group. "What will you do this week to help you get there?" another student asks her. Welcome to job club, a group of high school students with disabilities who meet on a weekly basis to plan their own lives, and direct their own futures.

The Springdale job club was developed by a local high school teacher and a Vocational Rehabilitation counselor who teamed up with a desire to create new services for youth in transition. This particular VR counselor had experience leading a job club for adults that focused on empowering people, providing them with the skills to make good decisions and take control of their lives. She felt that this model might also work well for a group of young people.

Armed with a few concepts about student empowerment and goal setting, the two started meeting with groups of students. At first the going was slow. Only a few students would show up each week, and from week to week you might see a completely different group. After a few months, a core group of students formed. These students were active in discussions, and willing to give input to make the job club better. Through their leadership, the job club became more "student-driven," and the essential features of job club were crystallized.

The job club has been meeting for almost five years now. The membership ebbs and flows, but it is consistently a place where students go to get the support they need to be successful in the community. One of the many "graduates" of job club said it best when he commented, "The program (job club) itself is based on what the person wants, not what everyone thinks is best for them. I have gained the skills and motivation that I need to find and hold a competitive job."

. . . .

Your first activity to establish a job club program should be to develop a brief program description that outlines its general structure, including goals and the students it is designed to serve. This written overview will be helpful as you lobby to get support for the program within the school and community. The information-gathering suggestions we offerred at the beginning of this section of the chapter will help you generate some initial ideas for this program description. Based on the experiences of YTP sites, we recommend six steps to develop a job club for students in transition:

1. obtain support within the schools;
2. obtain support from adult agency partners;

3. develop specific materials needed;

4. invite students to participate;

5. schedule regular job club meetings; and

6. monitor and evaluate the success of the program.

Obtain support within the schools

Before you can move ahead with implementing a job club you need to have support within the school. Set up a meeting with school administrators and other interested teachers to describe the proposed job club, and obtain their input and support for developing the program. Specific issues to discuss at this meeting include:

- Where and when will the job club meet?

- Who will coordinate and lead job club meetings?

- Which students will participate in job club? (You may want to include students who have dropped out of school, or are have already graduated.)

- How will students be referred to job club?

- What additional resource people need to be involved in job club?

This meeting is also a time to think about ways to tap the expertise of various school and agency staff as you build this program. At one site, high school teachers and administrators participated in mock interviews with students who were learning job seeking skills. Another site invited guest speakers from various community agencies to help the students understand how to access these programs.

Obtain support from adult agency partners

Most YTP sites have worked closely with staff from adult service agencies as they prepare students to transition into the world of work. Consider partnerships with the variety of federal, state, and local agencies that provide basic skills, continuing education, and/or job training to youth and adults (e.g., Vocational Rehabilitation, Adult and Family Services). Some programs may have existing job clubs that serve adults, while others may have staff with years of experience teaching job search skills on an individual basis. These local staff can be key resource people for you in developing the job club.

Develop specific materials

Develop a set of goals for the job club program, along with a general outline of content you want to address. There are many curricula available commercially that teach interviewing skills, resume writing, and other job search skills. In addition, several curriculum materials have been published recently that focus on student goal setting and person-centered planning. Depending on the goals you have for the program, and the skill level of your students, you may want to consider purchasing some of these curriculum resources. Or, you may want to design your own materials to meet the specific needs of your students.

Before you expend too much energy (and money) purchasing or developing curriculum materials though, remember that job club sessions should be flexible and based on the interests of your students. In one local job club, staff spent the first few job club sessions following a series of lesson plans they had created to teach specific job search skills. The students began complaining that this was "boring" and "too much like schoolwork." The staff decided to change the focus of job club from lesson plans to "topics." Students became responsible for generating topics, leading group discussions, and even inviting guest speakers of interest to them. These students also developed a list of key ingredients for job clubs. They are included in Appendix 2.9.

Invite students to participate

The specific students you invite to participate could vary, depending on the job club's goals. Some job clubs might consist of all of the students enrolled in a specific class; others could be a mixture of high school students, school drop-outs and students participating in postsecondary education. Still others could be a combination of students with and without special needs who are participating in structured work experiences as part of school-to-work activities. As part of the selection process, it is important to explain the purpose of the program to students and get an initial commitment from them to attend the meetings. Students should be given a written reminder of the time and place of meeting. School staff may also want to provide transportation to the meetings, especially if you are in an area with no reliable public transportation.

Schedule regular job club meetings

Job clubs can meet in a variety of places, including high school classrooms, community colleges, or even a meeting room at the local VR office. Consider using an off-campus location to reinforce the idea that this is an *adult* program designed to teach skills needed for independence. Schedule job club at a time that will be convenient for students who may be in school or working in the community. Most YTP sites in Oregon have found that late afternoon or early evening meetings seem to work best.

Job club meetings should be informal, interesting, and enjoyable for students and staff. Since job clubs often are held right after school, you may want to provide snacks and beverages. Plan special events such as field trips to visit job sites or guest speakers from the community to encourage participation. Each week you will want to include time for structured activities to teach or practice specific skills, as well as time for more informal student-driven discussion. An agenda for a typical job club meeting is included in Appendix 2.10.

Job club meetings are also an ideal time to practice goal setting. Some hints for helping students to identify goals are listed in Appendix 2.11. Each week, students can identify their short-term goal and also report on their goals from the previous week. By making this process public, students learn from and support each other as they strive to attain their goals. Students also are encouraged to write down their goals, keeping one copy for themselves and leaving one copy in a folder at job club. Recording goals helps motivate students because, as one student noted, "you can't change your mind, and you can't just forget your goal." Students that meet their weekly goal also receive a small reward from staff, such as a gift certificate for a free hamburger, or a free movie pass. Those that don't meet a goal are encouraged to try again or set a new more manageable goal. By setting small goals and attaining them students gain self-confidence. They also become comfortable with a process that they can use to manage transitions throughout their lives.

Evaluate the success of the program

The final step in developing any new program is to evaluate its impact. Job club staff can informally collect evaluation information from students and staff to determine the overall effectiveness of the program. Based on this feedback, staff can decide if the job club format should be revised, and whether or not to continue to offer a job club as an instructional option for students in transition.

Transition Class

The purpose of a transition class is to provide a forum for teaching skills needed to live and work in the community. These classes provide an opportunity for regular, structured instruction which is interactive, group-oriented, flexible, and most importantly relevant to the students. Transition classes are usually offered daily as part of the high school curriculum, although some classes can be scheduled to meet weekly at a community college. The content covered varies depending on the needs of the students, but in general these classes teach skills in vocational, personal–social, and independent living areas. The experiences of one YTP site with creating and using a transition class to address the school-to-work instruction needs of students are described in the following vignette.

· ·

Shakerton Transition Class

In Shakerton, staff knew from the beginning that their transition program was about more than "just finding jobs." As a team, they believed strongly in the importance of providing life skills instruction, and were convinced that they needed to develop a forum for teaching communication, decision making, and problem solving skills to the students in the program. The problem was logistics. The Youth Transition Program staff had been assigned to serve students across 3 large high schools. Some students were in school a full day, others were working and going to school half days, while others had already dropped out or graduated. What would be the best way to deliver instruction to this diverse group without creating scheduling havoc for the staff in the 3 high schools?

The answer was the community college. Working with the Community Education Coordinator at Shakerton Community College, the YTP teacher–coordinator put together an adult education class specifically for young adults in transition. The class, called "Choices and Challenges: Making Your Own Way After High School" was co-taught one night a week by the transition specialists, with some guidance and direction from the teacher–coordinator. The entire team developed the curriculum by pulling together various resource materials and organizing them into units that included the following topics: problem solving, decision making, communication, friendship, housing options, and transition planning. Students that were still enrolled in high school were able to earn an elective credit for the class; others enrolled as community education students.

Hosting a class at the community college had many benefits. For many students this was their first exposure to college life. The class was a fairly safe way to become comfortable with the community college campus and get to know some new people. Several of the graduates of the "Choices and Challenges" class have since gone on to enroll in other programs at the college. Since the YTP specialists were the primary instructors of the class, the weekly meetings gave them time to get to know the students and to begin to understand some of the issues in their lives. In the words of the teacher–coordinator "This created some very positive relationships between the specialists and the students. It was much different than just bumping into them in the halls at the high school."

As a side note, the class was also advertised as a continuing education course in the college bulletin, making it open to participation from any member of the community. Three students who were not part of the original YTP group enrolled in the class. One of these students was from a transition program in another school district. The other two community education students were simply interested in the topic—in fact one of them was in his 30s proving that you're never too old to learn some new life skills!

· ·

Your first activity to develop a transition class should be to devise a brief course description that outlines the general structure of the class, including goals of the program and the students it is designed to serve. This written overview will be helpful as you lobby to get support for the class within the school and community. The information-gathering suggestions we offered at the beginning of this section of the chapter will help you generate some initial ideas for this program description. We recommend five basic steps to develop a transition class:

1. obtain support for your concept within the school;

2. select students to participate;

3. develop specific materials needed;

4. teach class on a regular basis;

5. monitor and evaluate the success of the class.

Obtain support within the schools

Before you can move ahead with implementing the new class you need to have support within the school. Set up a meeting (or a series of meetings) with key school administrators to describe the proposed class and obtain their input and support for developing the program. Specific issues that should be resolved before you begin teaching the class include:

- Who will organize and teach the class?
- When and where will the class be held?
- Will it be a year-long class or for one term only?
- What student skills will be emphasized?
- What type of credit will students receive for participation?
- How will this class connect with other school-to-work activities ?
- What will the content of the curriculum be?

These up-front discussions to obtain administrative support and buy-in are critical to your later success. It is usually not easy to create a brand-new course offering within the structure of a high school, so you will need to be patient as you work to make changes in the system. You may want to collaborate with other staff who are responsible for developing school-to-work programs to see if you can create one course offering that will meet the needs of many students. Another strategy to consider is to revise an existing class, such as a career education course, to meet the specific needs of your students.

Select students to participate

You may decide to include all the students in your school-to-work program in the class or to limit enrollment to those students who need specific skills. Student participation also will be influenced by existing class and work schedules. As part of the selection process, it is important to explain the purpose of the class to students and get an initial commitment from them to attend.

Develop specific materials needed

There are many pre-packaged curriculums available that are designed to teach independent living, personal–social, and vocational skills to students in transition. Depending on the goals you have for this program and the skill level of your students, you may want to adopt or adapt existing curriculum materials or develop your own materials to meet the specific needs of your students.

Be aware that the class can include many aspects of life skills instruction. As a general rule, at-risk students will have a wide variety of needs when it comes to life skills instruction. Some may not be able to manage a checking account while others may need to learn how to secure their own apartment. It is also true that you may only have a year or less in which to deliver all this instruction (the "getting it all in a year" approach). Prioritizing the most important content will be critical. Remember to include student input as you set your priorities. A sample outline for a transition class developed by a local YTP site is included in Appendix 2.12.

Teach the class on a regular basis

In most YTP sites, classes meet daily for at least one hour as part of the regular high school schedule. Other scheduling options include meeting every other day as part of a block schedule or meeting once a week in the evening using an adult education model. You may also be able to offer several days a week of work-based learning alternating with a school-based transition class.

The class should be a mixture of structured instruction that focuses on specific goals identified by your students and more informal discussion and activities. Some classes have planned field trips to visit local businesses or community agencies. Other classes have included a series of speakers on transition-related topics. In general, staff have had the most success by obtaining student "buy-in" and input, facilitating student learning through hands-on instruction or role-playing, and by emphasizing problem solving and self-advocacy skills. An instructional philosophy that reflects these priorities is included in Appendix 2.13.

Evaluate the success of the class

The final step in developing any new program is to evaluate its impact. Staff should collect evaluation information from students to determine the overall effectiveness of the program. It is possible to evaluate the impact of the class by measuring student performance on specific skills or competencies, and/or by interviewing students to get their perception of the effectiveness of the class. Based on this feedback, staff should consider if the class needs to be revised and, ultimately, if it should be continued in subsequent school years. In the final analysis, the effectiveness of the class will be measured by whether your students are able to function independently as young adults in their community.

Independent Living Program

Independent living programs are designed to provide hands-on learning experiences that prepare students to live on their own. Programs are usually housed in off-campus apartments, but most do not include overnight accommodations. Rather, students can come to an apartment setting once or twice a week in the afternoon or early evening to meet with other students and practice the skills they are learning. For students in the independent living program, the apartment is a home-base, and the entire community becomes a classroom. The curriculum is determined by student needs and interests, and may include skills such as comparative shopping, cooking and nutrition, household maintenance, consumer knowledge, banking and budgeting, personal planning and time management, leisure activities, and interpersonal skills. Many students who complete these programs go on to live independently in their own apartments. In addition, many YTP sites that have developed apartment living programs have found that the apartment becomes a resource for conducting many of the other instructional options discussed in this chapter (e.g., job club meetings are held in the living room of the apartment). The experiences of one YTP site with creating and using an independent living program to address the school-to-work instruction needs of students are described in the following vignette.

· ·

Skinner City Independent Living Program

The small apartment was filled with people Friday afternoon. Adults in business attire and young people in jeans mingled while balancing plates of submarine sandwiches and soft drinks. One young woman proudly led tours of the place, pointing out the matching pink lamps in the living room and the new posters on the wall. This was the first open house for Skinner City's new independent living program, and the students were very excited about showing off their new place.

These students don't live here. Instead, the apartment is available during the daytime as a sort of "practice apartment" so they can learn the skills needed to live on their own. The entire program is designed to move students gradually through a three-phase process from classroom instruction to independent apartment living. The first phase of the program involves instruction at the high school in basic skills such as budgeting, banking, meal planning, and money management. In the second phase, students spend as many as two afternoons a week in the apartment "lab." At the apartment, students plan menus, prepare meals, wash clothes, clean the kitchen, and even pay the monthly bills. In the final phase of the program, students work individually with program staff to locate affordable housing and make the big move.

The apartment is part of a large complex complete with a swimming pool and recreation room. Two other selling points for this location were its proximity to a city bus line and grocery store. Monthly rent and initial deposits on the apartment are provided by a grant from the vocational rehabilitation division. Special education funds from the school district also are used to support the ongoing costs of the program. One of the staff members described the apartment program this way: "The focus of this program is to provide students with the skills and resources to become self-reliant adults. We asked the students what they needed to learn to live on their own and then built the program from there."

The students explained the effort that went into preparing for the open house. Over the last few weeks they visited all the second-hand stores in town, hunting for the best bargain furniture. After making a list of basic household supplies, they went shopping at the neighborhood grocery store. They even planned the party menu and invited teachers and other community agency representatives. During the open house, students took turns being the host or hostess, making sure everyone had plenty of good food and conversation. All in all, the open house was a successful event, and a step on the road to independent living.

. . . .

Your first activity to establish an independent living apartment program should be to develop a brief program description that outlines its general structure, including goals and the students it is designed to serve. This written overview will be helpful as you lobby to get support for the program within the school and community. The information-gathering suggestions we offered at the beginning of this section of the chapter will help you generate some initial ideas for this program description. It is also critical at this early planning stage that you involve other key players (both school and adult agencies) to discuss the feasibility of developing this type of program, and to get their input on the overall goals of the program. In our experience with YTP sites, we recommend 10 steps to develop an independent living program:

1. Obtain support for your concept within the school.

2. Obtain support from community agencies.

3. Obtain funding for the program.

4. Locate a site for providing off-campus instruction.

5. Arrange for personnel needed to provide instruction.

6. Develop instructional materials.

7. Select students to participate.

8. Purchase supplies/furnishings needed to set up the program.

9. Facilitate instruction in independent living skills.

10. Monitor and evaluate the success of the program.

Obtain support within the school

Before you can move ahead with developing an independent living program you need to have school administrative support. Set up a meeting with school administrators to describe the proposed program, and obtain their input and support. Specific issues that need to be discussed include:

- Is the district willing to support an off-campus program to teach independent living skills?

- What are the potential benefits to students as well as the risks/concerns to the school district?

- How will liability issues be addressed?

- What are potential sources of funding for this program?

- Who will coordinate and manage the program?

- Where will the program be housed?

- How will the program be staffed?

- What types of instruction will be offered?

- Will students receive school credit for participation?

All of these questions will certainly not be answered at this first meeting. It will take a substantial commitment of time and resources to develop this type of a program. Be sure to get an initial commitment from the school administration before you move ahead with the next steps in developing an independent living program.

Obtain support from community agencies

You will need to work closely with staff from adult service agencies in the community as you develop your independent living program. Your local vocational rehabilitation (VR) counselor can be a key resource person for you as you develop an independent living program. VR staff can refer you to other local service agencies who provide independent living services to adults with disabilities. These agencies can provide information and may be interested in developing a collaborative program. VR staff will also be critically important to you as you discuss options for funding this type of program.

Obtain funding for the program

School districts that have developed independent living programs have had to secure additional funding to start these programs. Funds are used to hire staff, rent a house or apartment, and purchase furniture and household supplies. There are several options for funding an independent program. YTP sites in Oregon have used a variety of small grants to secure start-up funds, including grants from local or state charitable foundations, service clubs, county agencies that administer state and federal housing funds, the state Department of Education, and the state vocational rehabilitation agency. Many sites have also secured a portion of their start-up costs from their school district. Most external grant sources require a written proposal that includes a program narrative and budget. These formats can vary greatly in detail and length. Once you have identified a potential funding source, call or write for their application packet. It also can be helpful to speak directly with a representative of the funding source to describe your need and idea and seek their input.

Locate a site to provide off-campus instruction

The next step is to search for an appropriate apartment or house for the program. Most sites have found one or two bedroom apartments to be affordable and fairly easy to find. The location should be accessible and within walking distance from either school or public transportation. As you investigate various possibilities, meet with the landlord to describe the purposes of your program, the students it will serve, and determine his/her level of support. Some programs have received a rent reduction in exchange for building or grounds maintenance. This provides yet another vocational training environment for students.

One of the biggest barriers to developing off-campus instruction is addressing the school district's liability for providing instruction off school property. After the program funding is secure, you will need to work with your school district administrators to address these liability issues. Meet with school district personnel responsible for risk management to discuss insurance coverage and issues encompassing student and classified staff supervision. You will also need to determine who will sign the lease or rental agreement.

Arrange for personnel

Most school districts that offer these services have found they needed to hire new staff to assume responsibility of developing and coordinating an independent living program. These new staff members are responsible for overall program development, direct instruction, and supervision of students. Independent living staff can be hired through the school district, or as direct contractors through an adult agency such as vocational rehabilitation. The person in this position should have good organizational skills, good teaching skills, and the ability to work in collaboration with staff from the school and adult agencies. A sample job description is included in Appendix 2.14.

Develop instructional materials

Many curricula are available commercially that teach independent living skills, such as money management, cooking and nutrition, and household management. If you are unsure of the content to include in your program, this is an ideal time to get input from the students. Tell them about the proposed apartment living program, and ask them what skills they think should be included. To help you get started with this discussion, a living skills competency list developed by students and staff at a local YTP site is include in Appendix 2.15.

After reviewing these materials and meeting with students to get their input, you should develop a set of goals for the program and a general outline of the content you plan to cover at each session. Depending on the program's goals and the skill level of your students, you may want to adapt existing materials, or develop your own materials designed to meet specific needs of your students.

Invite students to participate

You may decide to include all of the students in a specific class in the independent living program or to limit participation to those students who need training in specific skills. Most sites have found that these programs are most successful when they serve a fairly small group of students. Additional students can enter the program at a later time once the scheduling and staffing logistics have been ironed out. As part of the selection process, it is important to explain the purpose of the class to students and get an initial commitment from them to attend. You should also get input from the students about the best schedule for instruction. Most sites with independent living programs have found it is most effective to schedule small groups of students for blocks of time at the apartment. For example, some student groups meet twice weekly from 12:30 to 3:30 p.m.; others meet one evening a week from 3 to 6 p.m.

Purchase supplies/furnishings needed to set up the program

One of the first lessons that students in these programs have learned is how to furnish and purchase supplies needed to set up a household. A sample list of household items needed is included in Appendix 2.16. Student involvement may include painting walls, buying and refinishing furniture, or purchasing groceries to stock the cupboards. One program was able to get community businesses to donate paint, carpet, and even some used furniture. Involving students in this initial set-up process is very motivating and promotes the idea that this is "their place." Some sites have hosted open houses for school and community staff to show off the new living program.

Facilitate instruction in independent living skills

Independent living skills instruction should be balanced between time for structured instruction in specific skills, and open time for discussion and activities. Some programs follow a structured curriculum to ensure that students meet certain competencies; others use a more fluid approach of scheduling instruction around events or activities. Although much of the instruction will take place at the apartment, many sites also incorporate field trips to local businesses, community agencies, or recreational activities.

In all independent living programs, students have the opportunity to practice basic living skills such as planning menus, cooking meals, and cleaning up afterwards. Staff in these programs take on the role of facilitator, providing opportunities for learning, and guiding students as they make choices. Deciding who will cook and who will shop becomes a built in opportunity for instruction in the art of negotiation and compromise. An apartment program gives students a real world living experience, preparing them for the next step of living on their own.

Evaluate the success of the program

The final step in developing any new program is to evaluate its impact. Staff should collect evaluation information from students and staff to determine the overall effectiveness of the program. It is possible to evaluate the impact of the program by measuring student skill or competency levels, and/or by interviewing students for their opinion of the program's impact. Based on this feedback, staff should consider whether the program needs to be revised and, ultimately, whether it can be maintained in subsequent school years. In the final analysis, the effectiveness of the program will be measured by whether your students are able to function independently as young adults in their community.

APPENDIX 2.1
IDENTIFYING YOUR INTERESTS AND ABILITIES

Student Name: _____   Date: _____

Working

Interests (What do I like?)   **Abilities** (What do I do well?)

_____   _____

_____   _____

_____   _____

_____   _____

Continuing Education

Interests (What do I like?)   **Abilities** (What do I do well?)

_____   _____

_____   _____

_____   _____

_____   _____

Living in the Community

Interests (What do I like?)   **Abilities** (What do I do well?)

_____   _____

_____   _____

_____   _____

_____   _____

APPENDIX 2.2
VISUALIZE YOUR FUTURE: DECISIONS TO BE MADE

Where to Work?

Where to Live?

Leisure Activities?

Health Needs?

What do you want to do?

Continuing Education?

Friendships?

Transportation?

Civic Responsibilities?

(Continues)

What Do I Want to Do? Goal Summary Sheet

Student Name: _____ Date: _____

Work?

_____

_____

Continuing Education?

_____

_____

Living Arrangements?

_____

_____

Friendships?

_____

_____

Leisure Activities?

_____

_____

Transportation?

_____

_____

Health Needs?

_____

_____

Civic Responsibilities?

_____

_____

APPENDIX 2.3
TRANSITION SKILLS INVENTORY

Student Form

In order to help you think about your dreams for the future and your goals for next year, we want to get your opinion on how well you are doing now in four broad areas: (1) personal life; (2) jobs; (3) education and training; and (4) living on your own. In each of these areas, we have identified several skills for you to consider. After thinking about each skill, please use the rating scale shown below to indicate your sense of how well you are doing in that skill. You will notice that one of the rating possibilities allows you to indicate that a particular skill doesn't apply to you. For each of the skills described, please indicate your rating by placing an X on top of your choice.

(U)   I **usually** do this

(S)   I **sometimes** do this

(H)   I **hardly** ever do this

(DK)   I **don't know** how do this

	Usually Do	Sometimes Do	Hardly Ever	Don't Know
PERSONAL LIFE	(U)	(S)	(H)	(DK)
Communicating With Other People				
1. Do you look people right in the eye when you talk to them or when they talk to you?	(U)	(S)	(H)	(DK)
2. Do you listen carefully to other people when they talk to you and do you work hard at trying to understand what they are saying?	(U)	(S)	(H)	(DK)
3. Can you tell what other people are really thinking or feeling by the look on their face or the tone of their voice?	(U)	(S)	(H)	(DK)
4. When you are talking to other people, do you treat them with respect?	(U)	(S)	(H)	(DK)

(Continues)

	Usually Do	Sometimes Do	Hardly Ever	Don't Know
Relating to Authorities	(U)	(S)	(H)	(DK)
5. If you don't know what a teacher or employer wants you to do, do you ask questions?	(U)	(S)	(H)	(DK)
6. If you understand what a teacher or employer wants you to do, but you still need help, do you ask for help?	(U)	(S)	(H)	(DK)
7. If teachers or employers try to correct something you are doing, do you accept their help?	(U)	(S)	(H)	(DK)
8. If you think that a teacher or employer isn't treating you fairly, do you stand up for your rights without getting angry?	(U)	(S)	(H)	(DK)
Relating to Peers				
9. Do you get along well with people your own age?	(U)	(S)	(H)	(DK)
10. If something isn't going well between you and your friends, do you work it out?	(U)	(S)	(H)	(DK)
11. If you need something from a friend, do you ask for it?	(U)	(S)	(H)	(DK)
12. If somebody tries to take advantage of you, do you stand up for yourself and stop this from happening?	(U)	(S)	(H)	(DK)
Responsibility				
13. Do you complete your school assignments on time?	(U)	(S)	(H)	(DK)
14. Do you come to classes regularly and on time?	(U)	(S)	(H)	(DK)
15. Do you follow through on things that you tell your friends you will do?	(U)	(S)	(H)	(DK)
16. Do you follow through on things that you tell your parents you will do?	(U)	(S)	(H)	(DK)
Solving Problems				
17. When you have a problem, do you think of several different ways that you might solve the problem before you make up your mind?	(U)	(S)	(H)	(DK)
18. When you can't think of a good way to solve a problem, do you ask other people to help you think of some possibilities?	(U)	(S)	(H)	(DK)
19. After you have found some different ways to solve a problem, do you make your own decisions on what you are going to do?	(U)	(S)	(H)	(DK)

(Continues)

	Usually Do	Sometimes Do	Hardly Ever	Don't Know
Solving Problems **(Continued)**	(U)	(S)	(H)	(DK)
20. After you make a decision, do you follow through on doing what you have decided?	(U)	(S)	(H)	(DK)
Controlling your Anger				
21. When you get mad at someone, do you solve the problem without yelling?	(U)	(S)	(H)	(DK)
22. When you get mad at someone, do you figure out what to do without hurting that person?	(U)	(S)	(H)	(DK)
23. When you get mad at someone, do you figure out what to do without damaging property?	(U)	(S)	(H)	(DK)
24. When you get mad and can't figure out what to do, do you ask for help?	(U)	(S)	(H)	(DK)
Leisure Activities				
25. Do you have a hobby that allows you to spend time alone every week? Some examples are (1) using a computer, (2) playing a musical instrument, and (3) gardening.	(U)	(S)	(H)	(DK)
26. Do you do things for fun with other people every week? Some examples are (1) going out to eat, (2) going to a movie, (3) participating in a club, and (4) playing a team sport.	(U)	(S)	(H)	(DK)
27. Do you control the amount of television you watch each week so it doesn't interfere with other important things in your life?	(U)	(S)	(H)	(DK)
28. When you have just a little bit of spare time, do you find something interesting to do? Some examples include (1) reading a magazine, (2) playing a game, and (3) talking to a friend on the telephone.	(U)	(S)	(H)	(DK)

JOBS

Knowing about Jobs				
29. Can you explain the kinds of deductions that are taken away from a paycheck, like income tax and social security tax?	(U)	(S)	(H)	(DK)
30. Can you explain the kinds of benefits that come with some jobs, like health, vacation and retirement benefits?	(U)	(S)	(H)	(DK)

(Continues)

	Usually Do	Sometimes Do	Hardly Ever	Don't Know
Knowing about Jobs (Continued)	(U)	(S)	(H)	(DK)
31. Can you describe the different kinds of jobs available to young people in your community or state?	(U)	(S)	(H)	(DK)
32. Can you describe several different job possibilities that fit well with your skills and interests?	(U)	(S)	(H)	(DK)
Finding a Job				
33. Do you use different ways to hunt for jobs, like reading want ads and asking friends or family members for ideas?	(U)	(S)	(H)	(DK)
34. Do you prepare a good resume, with the right kinds of information in it?	(U)	(S)	(H)	(DK)
35. Do you complete job applications properly?	(U)	(S)	(H)	(DK)
36. Do you perform well in a job interview?	(U)	(S)	(H)	(DK)
Skills on the Job				
37. Do you arrive to work and leave the job on time?	(U)	(S)	(H)	(DK)
38. Is your employer satisfied with the amount of work you do and how well you do it?	(U)	(S)	(H)	(DK)
39. Do you follow the safety rules of your employer?	(U)	(S)	(H)	(DK)
40. Do you get along well with the other workers and your boss?	(U)	(S)	(H)	(DK)

EDUCATION AND TRAINING

	Usually Do	Sometimes Do	Hardly Ever	Don't Know
Reading				
41. Do you accurately read short phrases and sentences? Some examples are (1) short questions on a test, (2) restaurant menus, and (3) newspaper headlines.	(U)	(S)	(H)	(DK)
42. Do you accurately read short paragraphs? Some examples are (1) directions for cooking food, and (2) instructions for doing homework.	(U)	(S)	(H)	(DK)
43. Do you accurately read 2- or 3-page materials? Some examples are (1) newspaper, and (2) magazine articles.	(U)	(S)	(H)	(DK)
44. Do you accurately read difficult materials? Some examples are (1) textbooks, and (2) manuals for computers.	(U)	(S)	(H)	(DK)

(Continues)

	Usually Do	Sometimes Do	Hardly Ever	Don't Know
Writing	(U)	(S)	(H)	(DK)
45. Do you accurately write short sentences? Some examples are (1) grocery lists, and (2) short answers to questions to a test.	(U)	(S)	(H)	(DK)
46. Do you accurately write short paragraphs? Some examples are (1) a short letter to a friend, and (2) paragraph essay answers on a test.	(U)	(S)	(H)	(DK)
47. Do you accurately write 2- or 3-page assignments? Some examples are (1) an essay for an English class, and (2) a job application, including a letter describing your qualifications.	(U)	(S)	(H)	(DK)
48. Do you accurately write difficult papers such as research papers for a class?	(U)	(S)	(H)	(DK)
Math				
49. Do you add, subtract, multiply and divide whole numbers?	(U)	(S)	(H)	(DK)
50. Do you use basic units of measurement accurately? Some examples include measuring (1) weight in pounds and ounces, (2) length in inches and feet, and (3) time in hours, minutes and seconds.	(U)	(S)	(H)	(DK)
51. Do you add, subtract, multiply and divide numbers that include fractions or decimals?	(U)	(S)	(H)	(DK)
52. Do you use math skills to help solve problems in school or in the community? Examples include (1) doubling a recipe, (2) determining how much wood is needed to build a fence, and (3) developing a monthly budget.	(U)	(S)	(H)	(DK)

LIVING ON YOUR OWN

Self-Care

	Usually Do	Sometimes Do	Hardly Ever	Don't Know
53. Do you have good sleeping habits and get enough sleep?	(U)	(S)	(H)	(DK)
54. Do you take good care of yourself when you get sick?	(U)	(S)	(H)	(DK)
55. When you are having personal problems, do you go to friends or family members for help?	(U)	(S)	(H)	(DK)
56. Do you have good health habits, like avoiding tobacco, too much alcohol, or harmful drugs?	(U)	(S)	(H)	(DK)

(Continues)

	Usually Do	Sometimes Do	Hardly Ever	Don't Know
Nutrition and Fitness	(U)	(S)	(H)	(DK)
57. Do you eat well-balanced, healthy meals each day?	(U)	(S)	(H)	(DK)
58. Do you set a limit on the amount of junk food you eat each day?	(U)	(S)	(H)	(DK)
59. Do you maintain your weight at a good level?	(U)	(S)	(H)	(DK)
60. Do you exercise at least three times a week?	(U)	(S)	(H)	(DK)
Money Management				
61. Do you pay for things in stores without making mistakes? Some examples include (1) knowing if you have enough money to buy what you want, and (2) knowing if you get the correct change.	(U)	(S)	(H)	(DK)
62. Do you shop carefully and get things for good prices?	(U)	(S)	(H)	(DK)
63. Do you use a checking or savings account to manage your money?	(U)	(S)	(H)	(DK)
64. Do you budget your money well enough to pay for the things you want and need?	(U)	(S)	(H)	(DK)
Home Management				
65. Do you use basic tools like a hammer, pliers or screwdriver to fix things around the house?	(U)	(S)	(H)	(DK)
66. Do you help out with cleaning chores, like washing dishes and cleaning up your room every week?	(U)	(S)	(H)	(DK)
67. Do you help to prepare meals every week?	(U)	(S)	(H)	(DK)
68. Do you help to do the laundry every week?	(U)	(S)	(H)	(DK)
Community and Leisure Activities				
69. Do you use the telephone to get information about things you need, like finding out when a movie starts or making a doctor's appointment?	(U)	(S)	(H)	(DK)
70. Do you use some form of transportation to get around on your own, like a bus, a bicycle, or driving a car?	(U)	(S)	(H)	(DK)

(Continues)

	Usually Do	Sometimes Do	Hardly Ever	Don't Know
Community and Leisure Activities (Continued)	(U)	(S)	(H)	(DK)
71. Do you volunteer every week to do something that helps other people? Some examples include (1) getting food for hungry people, (2) collecting money for a charity, and (3) doing things for a volunteer group, such as the Red Cross or Special Olympics.	(U)	(S)	(H)	(DK)
72. Even if you can't vote, do you know about the people who are running for office each election day, and do you think about who you think should win?	(U)	(S)	(H)	(DK)

Personal Safety

	Usually Do	Sometimes Do	Hardly Ever	Don't Know
73. Do you know how to provide first aid for minor cuts, burns, bruises or sprains?	(U)	(S)	(H)	(DK)
74. Do you always use a seat belt in a car, or a helmet with a bicycle, motorcycle or roller blades?	(U)	(S)	(H)	(DK)
75. If a person asks you to do something that is dangerous, like hitchhiking, do you say "no"?	(U)	(S)	(H)	(DK)
76. If you need emergency help for a really bad sickness or injury, do you know how to get the help?	(U)	(S)	(H)	(DK)

APPENDIX 2.4
SUMMARY OF INSTRUCTIONAL NEEDS
AND PREFERENCES

Instructions: Fill in student's initials across the top. Then enter the specific skill areas that students have identified as *preferences* for instruction in the first column. For each skill area, indicate whether this is an instructional *need* by entering a check mark in the cell corresponding to each student. If the student does not need or want instruction in any area, leave the cell blank. Add the totals in each row to determine the highest priorities for instruction.

Skill Areas	Student Initials									Totals
Functional Academics:										
Vocational Skills:										

(Continues)

Skill Areas	Student Initials										Totals
Independent Living Skills:											
Personal/Social Skills:											

APPENDIX 2.5
MENTOR PROGRAM FACT SHEET

Course Overview

The Mentor Program is designed to pair youth with positive adult role models for the purpose of building self-esteem and confidence, developing skills, instilling a strong work ethic, and providing a variety of experiences and opportunities within workplaces in the community. This program will familiarize students with diverse employment opportunities available in the community, provide field experiences in the work place, and help direct the students toward career and educational goals.

Students Receive:

1. Program orientation that includes assessment of:
   - work environmental preferences
   - motivational preferences
   - personal values
2. Course book
3. Choice of project to be completed with mentor's assistance
4. One-half credit for completion of course book
5. Assistance from program administrator where need exists

Mentors Receive:

1. Training
2. Worker's compensation insurance coverage for student
3. Assistance and support from program administrator
4. Monthly newsletter
5. Monthly follow-up contact

More Facts:

- Mentors and students are matched according to the career interests of the student.

- Students must be between the ages of 16–21.

- Mentors spend a minimum of one hour per week with their students.

- Students do not receive pay for participating in the program.

APPENDIX 2.6
MENTOR PROGRAM PARTICIPANT RESPONSIBILITIES

Business Mentor Responsibilities

1. Interview student intern.

2. Develop with the student intern goals and working agreement describing what the intern will do, learn, and observe at the business.

3. Provide opportunities for the intern to observe and/or participate in decision-making activities at the work site.

4. Provide time to consult with the Mentor Program intern coordinator concerning the student at your convenience.

5. Notify the Mentor Program intern coordinator if problems occur.

6. Complete an evaluation of student growth and the program itself.

Student Intern Responsibilities

1. Interview with business mentor.

2. Develop with the business mentor goals and working agreement describing what you will do, learn, and observe at the business.

3. Notify the Mentor Program coordinator and the business mentor if you are sick or if an emergency occurs and you are unable to be at work.

4. Keep a time sheet of hours and days worked in your Mentor Program folder and at the work site.

5. Spend a minimum of 5 hours a week at the work place.

6. Be on time, honest, courteous, cooperative, healthy, well-groomed, wear appropriate clothing and be willing to learn.

7. Discuss problems and concerns with the Mentor Program intern coordinator and the business mentor.

8. Consult regularly with the Mentor Program intern coordinator and/or instructor.

(Continues)

9. Keep a journal recording activities and observations at the learning site.

10. Complete an evaluation of experience in Mentor Program.

11. Attend and participate in other school classes regularly.

APPENDIX 2.7
MENTORSHIP APPLICATION FORM

Name _____ Class of 19____

Address _____

Phone number _____ Date_____

Counselor _____

Do you have a job? _____ If so, what days? _____

Do you have transportation? _____

Do you participate in sports, clubs, etc? _____

Do you have a friend or relative in this career field? _____

List courses you have taken that will help with this mentorship.

_____

_____

_____

List hobbies, interests, etc. _____

_____

Describe past interest in subject and why you want to do a mentorship in this career area. _____

_____

_____

Parental Permission

I give my permission for my son/daughter to participate in the Mentorship Program.

_____   _____

Parent/Guardian   Date

APPENDIX 2.8
SUGGESTIONS FOR COMMUNITY MENTORS

Talking with Students About Your Work

Whether you are talking to many students or a few, whether they are young or in their teens, there are many things you can say to give students a realistic sense of the adult world.

Talk About People

Say what you personally get from your job and why you chose your line of work. Tell students about other people you work with and how your job relates to the community—who depends on your work and why. Mention others in the community who do similar kinds of work. Stress equality of career opportunities for both girls and boys, regardless of race or other stereotypes.

Talk About Skills

Relate your work to what students are learning and already know. Analyze your work ahead of time in terms of:

- What you read
- What you write
- How you listen
- How you use speech skills
- How you have to get along with others
- How you schedule your time
- How you need good health
- How you apply mathematics
- Kinds of thinking you do (problem solving, critical thinking, decision making)
- How you apply creative skills

Show students examples of what your job requires you to read, write, and compute. Students will be interested in the practical application of skills they are learning—and how these skills are used in a variety of occupations.

Talk About Tools, Materials, and Products

When possible, show students the actual tools and materials you use and products you produce.

APPENDIX 2.9
KEY INGREDIENTS OF JOB CLUB

1. Meet at a convenient time.

2. Meet at a convenient place.

3. Attendance should **not** be mandatory.

4. Provide snacks and beverages.

5. Allow the students to own the experience.

6. Have a minimal structure: short topic and goals.

APPENDIX 2.10
AGENDA FOR A JOB CLUB

Setting: Community Center
Time: 3:30–4:45 p.m.
Participants: Teacher and 6 students

1. **Introductions** (5 minutes)

    Participants state names and one personal strength or talent.

2. **Discussion or activity** (30 minutes)

    Members discuss a universal topic (e.g., finding a job or a place to live), a personal topic (e.g., dealing with rejection), or participate in a team building/recreational activity.

3. **Goal report** (20 minutes)

    Members report on progress toward meeting goals and provide proof of accomplishments.

4. **Rewards** (5 minutes)

    Members choose rewards for meeting individual goals.

5. **Set new goals** (10 minutes)

    Members state goals verbally and record them.

6. **Announcements of upcoming events/set topics for next week** (5 minutes)

APPENDIX 2.11
RECIPE FOR GOAL SETTING

1. All goals relate to a *long-range goal*.

2. All goals are *achievable* in one week.

3. All goals are *measurable and challenging*.

4. All goals are *public*.

5. All goals are *reported and recorded*.

6. All accomplishments are *rewarded*.

APPENDIX 2.12
TRANSITION CLASS OUTLINE

Suggested Priorities for Instruction

NOTE: There is no preconceived sequence to deliver this. Bridges must constantly be built across domains. The ongoing threads interwoven throughout instruction that create the bridges are problem solving, critical thinking, decision making, self-esteem, goal setting, community access, and personal time management.

1. Problem Solving
   a. stress management

2. Decision Making

3. Communication
   a. "I" messages
   b. paraphrasing

4. Housing Options
   a. budgeting
   b. purchasing
   c. household maintenance
   d. clothing maintenance
   e. transportation
   f. safety

5. Friendship
   a. strangers
   b. acquaintances
   c. friends

6. Transition Planning

7. Job Related Instruction

APPENDIX 2.13
INSTRUCTIONAL PHILOSOPHY STATEMENT

1. Learning is a lifelong activity and should be owned by the students involved in the learning process and not the teacher delivering the instruction.

2. The instruction delivered should therefore be eclectic, address the whole person, and be driven by an individual's desire to continue learning as opposed to being driven by the content chosen and owned by the teacher.

3. The concept of a teacher is therefore a misnomer. The teacher in this process becomes a guide, not a dictator. The teacher is responsible for exploring and offering activities, resources, and practical experiences to promote ownership of learning by the students. The teacher becomes a role model for the learning process.

4. The ability of an individual to react to a situation in life, to assess different response options, and to make responsible choices is central to this kind of instruction.

5. There is no such thing as the "right" choice. The opportunity to experience failure enhances the ability to explore different response options. Experiencing the consequences of certain choices (regardless of their "goodness" or "badness") is a critical component of this learning experience.

6. Instructional strategies need to be functionally based, relevant to an individual's real-life experiences, interactive, group-oriented, and ensure a safe environment to take risks and learn.

7. The *quality* of instruction is more important than the *quantity* of content delivered.

8. A problem-solving strategy incorporates the following specifics:
   a. Identify the problem.
   b. Brainstorm all possible solutions, no matter how silly.
   c. List all of the pros and cons of the possible solutions.
   d. Select a solution that best fits the individual's needs.
   e. Try it out, evaluate it, recycle to step (b) if it doesn't work.

APPENDIX 2.14
INDEPENDENT LIVING PROGRAM JOB DESCRIPTION

HOUSE MANAGER JOB DESCRIPTION
Part-time position, 30 hours a week
Hours: 4:30 pm to 10:30 pm

Duties

1. Enforce house rules.
2. Coordinate household chores among residents.
3. Provide resident support/encourage them in their independent living goals.
4. Coordinate with other agencies or support service providers for repairs or maintenance, as needed.
5. Assist with shopping for food for individual residents if necessary.
6. Assist with shopping for shared household products such as cleaning supplies.
7. Pro-rate and facilitate payment of monthly phone bill.
8. Facilitate weekly house business meeting with residents.
9. Keep a house/program log for each shift.
10. Keep case file notes for each individual resident if significant and necessary.
11. Coordinate with relief and respite staff each week.
12. Arrange and participate in a weekly leisure or recreation activity for the residents.

Qualifications

Experience with group facilitation, good communication skills, experience with or knowledge of mediation and conflict resolution techniques.

APPENDIX 2.15
INDEPENDENT LIVING SKILLS COMPETENCIES

It is the mission of the Youth Transition Program staff to maximize the potential of clients to the optimum of their individual abilities and to ensure a Living Skills competency level allowing each client to have an independent life in the community. Supporting this mission are goals designed to provide hands-on experiences leading to competency levels sufficient to secure and maintain employment, manage fiscal affairs, secure and maintain a residence, and interact appropriately on an interpersonal level with other people. Each of the goals are represented by competency indicators measured against a sequenced, formal curriculum and a community-based living skills practicum of hands-on experiences.

Goal 1

Each client will develop adequate, measured competency in skills designed to secure and maintain employment appropriate to the client's ability and aptitude.

The client will:

1.1 Research the field of interest through mentorship and shadowing experiences.
1.2 Prepare a proper resume.
1.3 Seek available employment opportunities by:
>   reading classified advertisements,
>   personally inquiring about jobs,
>   applying at the Employment Division, and
>   sending employment applications.
1.4 Practice proper grooming and dress.
1.5 Interview appropriately for jobs.

Goal 2

Each client will obtain a minimum, measured competency level in maintaining a residential household.

The client will:

2.1 Look for affordable housing.
2.2 Complete a rental agreement.
2.3 Complete and submit a HUD application form.
2.4 Apply for utilities hook-up.
2.5 Rent or purchase household furnishings.
2.6 Develop and maintain chore schedules.
2.7 Learn and apply techniques for routine household maintenance.

Goal 3

Each client will obtain the skills necessary to manage money in daily living.

The client will:

3.1 Make lists of necessary purchases prior to shopping.
3.2 Shop for groceries for a specific meal.
3.3 Shop for groceries for one week's meals.
3.4 Open a checking account at a local bank.
3.5 Open a savings account at a local bank.
3.6 Pay bills using a checking account.
3.7 Demonstrate the ability to do effective comparative shopping.

Goal 4

Each client will demonstrate an ability to interact appropriately with other people in the community, on the job, and in recreational situations.

The client will:

4.1 Communicate clearly when asking questions of others.
4.2 Respond clearly and politely when answering questions.
4.3 Show respect for the ideas of others.
4.4 Ask for clarification when a question or statement is not understood.
4.5 Develop and implement a plan for solving conflicts.
4.6 Develop methods for managing stressful situations.
4.7 Use appropriate group discussion skills.
4.8 Develop and practice self-assertiveness.

APPENDIX 2.16
INDEPENDENT LIVING PROGRAM—
HOUSEHOLD ITEMS NEEDED

Bathroom
Bathtub Mat
Rags
Rug
Scouring Powder
Sponges
Toilet Bowl Cleaner
Toilet Brush
Toilet Paper
Towels
Tub & Tile Cleaner
Wash Cloths
Wastebasket
Window Cleaner

Bedroom
Bed
Bedspread
Blankets
Dresser
Hangers
Lamps
Mattress Pad
Nightstand
Pillows
Rugs
Sheet and Pillowcases
Wastebasket

Emergency Equipment
Batteries
Emergency Numbers
Fire Extinguishers
First Aid Kit
Smoke Detectors
Working Flashlight

Kitchen
Baking Soda
Broom
Butcher Knife
Can Opener
Canister Set
Cookie Sheet
Cooking Utensils
Cutting Board
Dish Cloths
Dish Towels
Dishes
Drinking Glasses
Dust Pan
Electric Mixer
Flour, Sugar, and Salt
Food for 1 Week
Garbage Can
Knives
Measuring Cups and Spoons
Menus
Microwave
Mixing Bowls
Mop
Other Staples
Oven Mitts
Pancake Turner
Paring Knife
Pitcher
Pot Holders
Pots and Pans
Salt and Pepper Shakers
Silverware
Spices
Table and Chairs
Teapot
Timer
Toaster

Living Room
Chairs
Coffee Table
Couch
End Tables
Lamps
Television

Miscellaneous
Bucket
Clock
Clothes Hamper
Fan
Iron
Ironing Board
Light bulbs
Placemats
Radio
Scales
Scrub Brush
Tablecloth
Vacuum Cleaner

career changes and the need for lifelong learning grow, and as more and more older people engage in volunteer and paid work to provide both emotional and financial incentives during their "retirement" years.

What hasn't changed is the fundamental importance of work in our lives. As the chapter opening quotes suggest, human beings have a *need* to work, a *need* to be engaged in activities that are productive and personally meaningful. In American society, work provides a basic source for financial support and self-esteem, and a means for full participation in community life. And yet, as the outcome data we reviewed in Chapter 1 document, many individuals with disabilities and other special needs have yet to realize these benefits of work. In its national study of Americans with disabilities, the National Organization on Disability (1994) concluded that not working is perhaps the truest definition of what it means to be disabled. There are many reasons why people with disabilities and other special needs are not participating fully in the economic mainstream of society. All of them require attention. Some of them can be addressed through well-designed school-to-work programs.

Creating work-based learning and employment opportunities for youth is at the core of school-to-work transition programs being developed in communities across the country. Work-based learning opportunities provide students with "real world" experiences that allow them to apply the academic and occupational knowledge they acquire in school and learn the general workplace competencies valued by employers (e.g., positive work habits, job-related social and communication skills). Under the best circumstances these experiences help all youth, including special needs youth, gain greater appreciation for the relationship between education and earning power, and greater understanding of themselves and the world of work. And they provide youth with opportunities to acquire skills and learn the value of a "job well done."

Creating work-based learning and employment opportunities for special needs youth requires an understanding of the obstacles that many of these youth face in the school-to-community transition process. Our direct experience, and the research literature (e.g., Carnegie Council on Adolescent Development, 1995; Dryfoos, 1990; Siegel, Robert, Greener, Meyer, Halloran, & Gaylord, 1993; William T. Grant Foundation, 1988), suggests that many youth with special needs will enter school-to-work programs with limited or no previous work history. Others will have had a succession of short-term, and perhaps negative, job experiences. As a consequence, most will have a limited understanding of themselves (e.g., their interests, abilities, and values) and the world of work—two components essential to effective career planning. In addition, many will need instruction and support with general work place competencies (e.g., positive work habits, job-related social and communication skills).

At the same time, the living situations of many special needs youth require that they secure and maintain paid employment. Some youth provide partial or full support for their families. Still others must support themselves, often for reasons such as homelessness, a transient living situation, parenting responsibilities, or the need to move out because of difficult or unstable family circumstances. It's not easy to secure and maintain paid employment under these circumstances. As a consequence, many youth will need immediate support to stabilize their living situation, and ongoing instruction in the life skills necessary to maintain a home and live in the community. Finally, some special needs youth will enter school-to-work programs with weak, unstable, or negative support structures, and a history of sporadic attendance patterns, or of not completing previous programs they have begun.

Providing work-based learning and employment opportunities under these circumstances can be challenging. Programs must provide a wide range of *paid* work-based learning options in order for students to explore various occupations and work environments, learn greater career awareness and workplace competencies, *and* earn enough money to help support themselves or their families. This chapter describes two sets of strategies for creating employment opportunities for youth, including strategies for creating: (a) paid work placements with individual employers in the community and (b) programmatic options for building students' work skills and ethic. These strategies will provide a wide range of opportunities for students to acquire the employment skills that you identify with them as important, and for your program to build collaborative work-based experiences within your school and community.

It should be clear, however, from the previous discussion on the obstacles that confront many youth with special needs that the ideas and strategies described in this chapter do not stand alone. If students' work-based experiences are to have real educational value, they must be structured by an individualized career/transition plan that makes explicit to the student the connection between work, school, and their postschool goals. Similarly, students must have instruction and support to address the broader life skill issues that will enhance or impede their ability to proceed and benefit from a path of paid work experiences. The ideas and strategies described in Chapter 2 address these issues. Together, these two chapters outline concepts and procedures for helping students develop meaningful work skills and interests, and connect these experiences to other aspects of their lives both in and out of school.

CREATING EMPLOYMENT OPPORTUNITIES WITH INDIVIDUAL EMPLOYERS

Creating employment opportunities for students will be a fundamental aspect of your program. Students will be seeking employment with individual community employers throughout the program. Among the final services students receive from your program may be assistance to secure a career-entry position with an employer in the community. The procedures described in this section are intended to help you accomplish three goals:

1. Develop ongoing relationships with community employers who will be supportive of your school-to-work efforts.

2. Achieve good student/job matches in order to provide meaningful, paid jobs that are consistent with student qualifications and interests.

3. Provide students with job-related support that will promote self-determination, job satisfaction and retention, and quality of life.

The ideas and strategies described in the section titled, "Building Relationships and Recruiting Employers," are designed to help you accomplish the first goal. During this step, the employment resources of the community are identified and on-going contacts are developed. It is important at this stage to become familiar with area employers, business trends, and employment opportunities. The outcome of employer recruitment is a pool of community employers who are supportive of your program. Only some of these employers will actually hire students. Others will support the program in various ways, such as allowing students to visit their business and observe or job shadow, offering their place of business as a work experience site, talking with students about their business as part of a class, or serving as volunteer mentors with specific individual students. Think of this phase as laying the groundwork for solid relationships within the business community that will pay off in dividends down the road for the youth served by your program.

The procedures described under "Matching Students and Job Possibilities" are designed to accomplish the second goal. Contacts with employers during this phase are more in-depth than the ones made to determine the general interest of an employer. The characteristics and demands of *specific* jobs are analyzed, and this information is matched against the interests and abilities of specific students. Students are provided with the assistance necessary to investigate and pursue appropriate jobs. The outcome of this phase is the placement of students in a paid job in which they are interested and for which they are qualified. The procedures described in the section titled, "Providing Job Training and Support," are designed to help you accomplish the third goal. This phase includes both the initial training required to teach the job to the student and the follow-along support strategies required to help the student maintain job success and satisfaction. The outcome of the job training and support phase is a successful job placement. The student should be meeting the goals outlined in his/her transition plan and making progress toward independent functioning on the job.

The ideas and strategies described in this section are based on several assumptions about job development for youth with special needs.

- *Employers are usually willing to be flexible about the "people side" of managing a business.* The employers you will be working with most likely will be very good at what they do for a living (e.g., banking, sheet metal fabrication, auto body repair)—they have to be if they are going to stay in business and prosper. That does not mean they are experts in other aspects of running a business (e.g., hiring, training, and supporting employees) that are central to your success in helping youth learn general workplace competencies and acquire and maintain paid employment. In fact, with time and the experience of developing jobs for students with varying interests and abilities, you will become an expert in these issues and that will be one of the more valuable services you have to offer the business community.

- *Employers are usually willing to be flexible about job requirements.* It's easy to assume that a clear logic and well thought out analysis lies behind the way jobs are designed, job qualifications are established, and job descriptions are written. This may be true in some cases, but often job requirements are the way they are because "it has always been done that way." Similarly, it's easy to assume that employers will be wary of discussing and exploring "reasonable accommodations" for youth with special needs. But, look in virtually any work setting and you will see accommodations of one kind or another—a bigger computer screen for one employee to reduce eye strain, a telephone headset for another to allow greater productivity or reduce neck strain. Employers make accommodations all the time to enhance productivity, reduce work-related injuries, or both. The job analysis skills gained through your job development experiences, coupled with creativity and knowledge about creating job accommodations, will be one of the more valuable support services you offer and will greatly increase the range of better-paying jobs available to youth with special needs.

• *Job development for special needs youth should foster integration and self-determination.* As the assumptions above imply, job developers have a number of tools and services to offer employers across all aspects of job development—employee recruitment, job matching, and job training and support. It can be tempting to use these tools and resources in ways that create "special" employment situations for youth in work sites (e.g., circumventing the typical way in which most employees apply and interview for jobs) or that take responsibility away from supervisors or co-workers to ensure that youth have the training and support they require to succeed. Similarly, it is easy to do too much for students in the interest of achieving the best job situation possible. Be aware of these issues. It is in students' long-term interests to create employment opportunities for youth that are as similar as possible to other employees in the work site and that foster integration and self-determination. To the extent possible allow on-site supervisors and co-workers to take responsibility for ensuring that youth have a successful learning and employment experience. And, provide maximum opportunities for students to take an active role across all of these activities.

• *Creating employment opportunities for special needs youth takes time and resources.* Youth with special needs can learn career awareness and workplace competencies and experience success in higher skill, higher wage jobs, but only if they have support to address the personal, environmental, and educational obtacles that often impede transition success for these youth. School-to-work programs that require youth to create work-based learning and employment opportunities without adequate support, or that require youth to seek out staff to receive work-related instruction and support services, will not provide real opportunities for special needs youth to succeed. This is especially true for youth who have a history of sporadic attendance, of not completing programs they have begun, or who lack a stable, positive support structure. The ideas and strategies described next assume there will be sufficient staff time and resources to provide this individualized support.

Build Relationships with Employers

Gather labor market information for your community

Gather information on both the current and the projected job market. What jobs currently exist in the community? What jobs or industry sectors are projected to decline over the next five years? Which ones are projected to increase? Are there any plans to attract new industry to the community?

Gathering this information is not a one-time event. You will want to review and update it on a regular basis—perhaps annually depending on how dynamic the employment base is in your community. There are several ways to gather this information.

Explore whether any formal labor market studies exist for your community or region. State Employment or Economic Development Departments often will conduct studies that are analyzed by industry sector and geographical region of the state. These agencies may or may not have reports for individual communities, but many are willing to conduct customized searches of their databases. Chambers of Commerce or local business associations also conduct their own studies. With the availability of electronic databases and connectivity to local and state agencies through the Internet, it is increasingly likely that program staff will be able to search directly for locally relevant labor market information. There are also many less formal strategies for identifying labor market status and trends in your community. The business section of your newspaper can contain a wealth of information about current and projected business trends. Read this section of the paper regularly, along with the section that lists new business licenses. Local radio and television stations that host "business beat" segments can also provide useful information. Find out when these segments are broadcast and listen to them. New businesses in the community, and existing businesses that are expanding, adding additional product lines, or adding new employees are often featured in these sources.

These various strategies will help you stay abreast of the current and future employment opportunities that are advertised or communicated to the community, and help you identify specific opportunities for individual students. It is estimated, however, that the vast majority of employment opportunities occur in the "hidden job market." More often than many people realize, jobs come open and are filled without any formal advertisement. A job opening occurs or is anticipated. The supervisor or small business owner discusses the opening with current employees, co-workers, or other members of his/her business "network." A referral is made, and the position is filled. As we describe later, much of job development involves "being at the rabbit hole when the rabbit comes up." Accessing the hidden job market requires that you be involved in the same networking activities as other business people. Look for opportunities to participate in service clubs such as the Active 20/30 or the Kiwanas. Consider joining organizations such as the Toastmasters Club to work on your speaking skills and meet local business people with the same goal.

Finally, meet and stay connected with other job developers in your community. There may be several other agencies or programs that help youth or adults find community employment. For example, your local Employment Division may have a particularly strong youth employment program, private non-profit agencies in the community may offer employment training programs, or specific occupational skill training programs might exist at the local community college. All of the personnel in these programs are potential resources for locally relevant labor market information. In many communities, local job developers have created a job developers network to share labor market information and create a coordinated job development approach with the business community.

Develop a systematic approach for contacting employers

In this step you need to make some decisions about *how* you will be contacting employers. Decide how much time you have each week to devote to job development activities, and how you plan to divide your energies between general marketing or networking activities (such as making group presentations) and contacting individual employers.

Presentations about your program to local organizations such as the Chamber of Commerce and other business and service organizations can be a cost-effective way to market your program within the business community and make face-to-face contact with a variety of community and business leaders. If you choose this approach, plan a brief presentation that outlines the services provided by your program and describes how schools and the business community can develop partnerships to better prepare students for life in the community. You may need to differentiate your programs from other existing employment programs in the community. Avoid using educational jargon to describe the program, and use *real* examples of students to illustrate your points. As your program grows, and you have "success" stories to tell about the positive impact the program has had upon students and employers, consider presenting this information through multimedia formats (e.g., slide/sound or video presentations). These formats can be effective and powerful additions to your verbal presentation. To close your presentation, give audience members options for how they can participate in your program (e.g., job shadowing or work experience sites, mentoring relationships, field trip or informational interview sites, etc.). Hand out any written information you have, such as a program brochure, and collect the names of people who are interested in receiving further information. These ongoing contacts with business people will give your program credibility in the community and also assure later sources for specific job leads.

There are two basic strategies you can use to contact individual employers: informational interviews and "cold calls." With informational interviews, you schedule specific times to meet with employers and present them with information about your program. Cold calls involve dropping-in on various places of business, finding out about possible job openings, and perhaps leaving some written information about your program. Sometimes you can use a cold-call to arrange a later in-depth interview with an employer. Most local sites in the Youth Transition Program (YTP) network have found that a combination of these two approaches are most effective. Other YTP sites have found that they prefer contacting employers when they have a particular student in mind and a specific vocational focus for that student. No matter which approach you use, *it is very important to listen carefully to what the employer wants and needs.* Employers frequently state that they welcome appropriate training and support (some of the business services you will be offering as you job develop) but express a strong aversion to inflexible and bureaucratic procedures inherent to many vocational programs.

Whatever strategies you use, create a written plan for contacting employers that includes specific goals and timelines (e.g., contact at least 10 employers per week, or conduct one marketing presentation each month). Develop a list of potential employers to contact. Review the labor market information you gathered. Use Chamber of Commerce listings, the telephone book, or the classified section of your local newspaper to locate individual employers in the market areas you are targeting. You will probably have good luck with employers who have had work experience students or who have hired persons with disabilities in the past. Once you've identified a list of potential employers, group them either by type of jobs offered or geographic location. These groupings will make it easier for you to plan your job search contacts. Remember that this is a working plan and should be adjusted as needed. It is important to establish a general plan to help you get started.

Design a system for maintaining employer contact information. You will be contacting many potential employers, and it will be important to maintain a record of these contacts. You will want to develop a well-organized resource bank of potential employers. This information can be organized in paper form using file folders, or if you have access to a computer you can store the same information in a database. Suggestions for designing an Employer Contact System are included in Appendix 3.1. Establishing a systematic approach for managing employer contact information will help you sort out when to re-contact interested employers and when to purge those employers "you can never get to first base with."

Begin the process of contacting employers in your community

There is no substitute for direct and regular contact with individual employers if your goal is to build relationships with the business community. Before you actually set out to meet with potential employers, you will want to prepare materials that you can leave at the various businesses you contact. Information to be developed might include: (a) a description of the purposes and services offered by your program, (b) identification of the benefits of program participation for employers and students, (c) a listing of local employers who have participated in the program and statements (or a short letter) of endorsement from one or more of these employers (as soon as these are available), and (d) identification of an address and phone number for the program for employers wishing further information. With the general availability of desktop publishing software, you can easily present much of this information in a simple, attractive brochure. An example of a brochure created by a local YTP site is included in Appendix 3.2. In addition to this information, program staff making personal calls on employers should have a business card. Make sure that your business cards and marketing materials look professional. A frequent complaint of many employers is the lack of professionalism apparent in many of the materials they receive from educators.

If you are planning to schedule informational interviews with selected companies you will need to do some additional groundwork. First, find out who to contact at the company and who the real decision maker is concerning employment. Often, this person is not in the Human Resources Department, but may instead be an "on-line" supervisor or mid-level manager. Then gather as much background information on the company (e.g., size, product, reputation) as you can. You can get this information from the Chamber of Commerce or from other local business people. You may also want to send out a letter of introduction that describes your program and states your intentions to call the employer soon to set up an appointment (see Appendix 3.3 for a sample letter of introduction).

At this point you are ready to visit business sites and meet with employers. Since this is your initial contact with the employer, it is important that you are well prepared. Dress as you would for a job interview, and be sure to have information about your program with you. Employers are busy people, so plan to spend about 30 minutes for this interview. You will spend even less time if you are making a cold-call. Most importantly, *know what you want to get out of this visit.* What are your goals for this visit? To introduce your program? To find out more about this industry? To determine this employer's awareness of the need for youth job training programs in the community, and his/her interest in participating at some level? To negotiate a possible placement for one or more students? To the extent it is consistent with your goals for this visit, gather information needed to complete a preliminary evaluation of the potential of this worksite as a place of employment for your students. A sample Site Screening Form is included in Appendix 3.4. Finally, determine the employer's level of interest in participating in your program. Give the employer several options for participation, including:

- allowing students to visit the business to observe or job shadow with one or more employees,
- talking with students about their business as part of a class or job club,
- serving as a volunteer mentor with a specific individual student,
- serving as a work experience site for students, and
- hiring students as paid employees.

If the employer is interested in participating, determine which options the employer is currently interested in and make follow-up arrangements. If the employer is not currently interested or is unsure about participating at this time, close the conversation by suggesting that the employer contact you with any questions or if the employment situation changes. Also ask if you might stop by at a future date to check on employment possibilities as you work with other employers in this area. As you leave, thank the employer for taking the time to talk with you, and leave a business card with your name and number.

Document the employers you contacted and the outcomes of your visit using your Employer Contact System. First, document in your Employer Contact files any contacts you made, even if the employer is not currently interested in the program. Later, you will update this card if this employer chooses to interview or hire one of your students. Next, review your Site Screening Forms, and make a list of employers who are interested in participating with your program in one way or another. As you are looking at this information you will also want to answer the bottom line question, "Is this a potential employer for my students?" Remember that you may meet some employers who want to hire your students, but for one reason or another, you don't think the work site is a good one. Don't be afraid to screen out these employers.

Send a thank you letter to every employer contacted. Since every employer contacted may someday participate in your program, it is important to maintain positive working relationships with all of them. Let them know in writing that you appreciate the time they took from their schedules to meet with you. Send a standard employer thank you letter to employers you don't intend to work with at this time. For employers you plan to develop further, send an employer thank you letter that outlines future involvement with your program. A sample letter that contains these options is included in Appendix 3.5.

Match Students and Job Possibilities

Help students prepare for job search activities

There are four general activities students should complete in order to conduct an effective job search. They should have a well-designed resume, know how to complete job applications accurately and neatly, know how to complete an effective job interview, and they should have a specific job search plan. These activities can be completed by students with one-to-one assistance from a staff member or a peer who possesses these skills, or they can be addressed through many of the instructional options described in Chapter 2 (e.g., job club, transition class, mentorship program).

Before students begin an active job search they should have a completed resume. Students should take responsibility for this activity to the extent possible. The resume worksheet included in Appendix 3.6 can be used to help the student gather and organize the critical information to be included on the resume. Students who are comfortable using a computer word processing program can create their own resumes using the worksheet as a guide. As an alternative, staff can help students create their resumes, or help them identify and secure professional help to have their resumes developed by individuals or companies that are in the business of creating "polished" resumes. This latter strategy is one that many people use, and certainly one that could be useful to students who are not computer proficient.

Students need to know how to fill out job applications neatly and accurately. The written job application gives an employer a first impression of the student as a potential employee, and is often the only opportunity a student will have to present his/her qualifications to an employer. Teach students how to transfer the information contained in their resumes to job applications by completing a series of practice applications. Emphasize to students the importance of submitting neat and complete job applications. As part of the process of completing job applications, you will want to verify that students have the necessary paperwork to document their eligibility for employment in the United States (the Employment Eligibility Verification I-9 Form), and help them obtain copies of any special documentation (e.g., a birth certificate) that they will need to be hired.

Interviewing for jobs is a skill not an art, and it is a skill that many youth (and adults) can learn and refine. A list of 12 commonly asked interview questions is included in Appendix 3.7. Review the interview questions with students and discuss appropriate responses to each one. Have the students write down answers on the worksheet provided, and then give them opportunities to orally practice their answers. Provide feedback to students on the content of their answers, as well as how they present themselves (e.g., their posture, smile, and extent to which they maintain eye contact with the interviewer). After students have practiced their skills on their own, they should then go through a series of "mock" interviews where they practice entering a room, greeting an employer, answering a series of questions, and closing the interview. As a final test of their interview skills, you may want to arrange for a local business person to come into your classroom and interview students.

Finally, help students develop a specific job search plan. Although program staff will be actively involved in developing job leads, each student also should have specific job search responsibilities. Students may be responsible for developing a list of potential employers to contact based on their identified job interests, or for completing a certain number of job applications each week. Students can use the Job Contact Sheet included in Appendix 3.8 to organize and record their job search activities. Program staff should meet regularly with students to review progress, share information on possible job openings, and set new job search goals. All things considered, students will have a higher probability of success in seeking and securing employment if they learn and practice effective strategies to find, get, and keep their own jobs rather than having it done for them.

*Help students compare their work experiences/interests
to various job possibilities*

Review and discuss with students information on their work experiences
and interests in order to begin the process of identifying desirable employment options. Much of this information will already be available from the
information that was gathered at the time the student entered the program,
and from the planning activities the student engaged in to identify interests
and abilities and set goals for participation in the program. In addition, discuss any specific issues or preferences that could impact the kind of job the
student would accept (e.g., how many hours the student can work each
week, the type of transportation that will be used to get to work).

Using this information as a general guide, identify several job possibilities
that are currently available in the community. Start by reviewing information
in your employer contact files. Identify potential employers in the general
occupational areas of interest to the student. For each employer you contact,
find out if they have any current or projected job openings, and if they are
willing to meet with you to discuss the placement of a specific student. You
may also need to expand beyond the employers already listed in your files. If
so, use other resources for job leads such as newspaper want ads, information
from the Employment Division, and your network of contacts in the community. Students should be involved in these activities, and may even have
contacts through family, neighbors, or friends that could be pursued.

After you identify employers with potential job openings, arrange to
visit each place of business to gather information about job requirements
and employer expectations. You can collect this information by asking
questions of the employer and also by directly observing the job. Keep in
mind that there may be more than one type of job available at any single
site. Interview the employer about the jobs available, noting the work hours
required and the job duties. If possible, observe the jobs that may be available. Note any special skills required, such as filling out forms, operating
complex machinery, or running a cash register. You will want to have a simple, straightforward way of documenting the information you obtain about
prospective jobs. This will be essential for communicating critical information to students and other staff, and for maintaining a written record of
contacts with an employer for other staff who may work with this employer
in the future. A sample Job Summary Form is included in Appendix 3.9.

Provide students with instruction and support to evaluate the match
between their work abilities and interests and the requirements of various
job possibilities. Students should play a major role in planning for the job

placement, regardless of whether it is the first work experience for the student or it is the student's final job upon leaving the program. Equally important is the need for a student-directed career plan to guide decisions about the desirability of individual job placements. Organize and summarize this information in a manner that will allow you to review and discuss this information with the student.

Help students evaluate the match between their abilities and interests and the requirements and opportunities of the various job possibilities that have been identified. Your short-term goal is to help students identify and acquire a paid job that is consistent with their interests and abilities and their long-range goals, that provides opportunities to learn important skills, and that provides satisfaction. Your long-term goal is to help students learn more about themselves and the world of work through these experiences—to learn the career awareness knowledge and skills that will allow them to identify and acquire meaningful, satisfying employment when your support is no longer available to them. Encouraging students to take an active role in this process, and providing them with instruction and support to learn these skills, will accomplish both your short-term and long-term goals.

Help students apply and interview with potential employers

Through your job development activities, as well as the job search efforts of your students, you will probably identify a variety of employers who have suitable job openings. Most employers will require the student to complete a job application, and some may even request a resume. Help students obtain and complete a presentable, competitive application. Use this opportunity to reinforce the importance of completing applications in a way that demonstrates desirable work qualities such as neatness, attention to detail, and thoroughness. You might also point out that employers often use the information contained in applications to develop interview questions that explore work history, skills, and qualifications. Help students identify these possible areas and prepare possible responses.

Review guidelines for conducting a successful job interview. Confirm that the student has reliable transportation and knows how to get to the employment site. Most students will want to interview with employers without staff present, and most will be able to do so successfully with the instruction and support they have received. Some students, however, may need transportation or may need a staff member present at the interview. You may need to sit in on the interview if you feel the student is not ready to answer questions independently, or if you feel you need to be available to answer the employer's questions about your program. Observing the interview will allow you to evaluate whether the student needs to practice his or her interviewing skills.

Students should document each interview and maintain a current, accurate job search plan. This practice will also provide them with notes to reference later in the search process. These notes can be recorded on the Job Contact Sheet or whatever strategy they are using to structure their job search process. For similar reasons, program staff will want to note the date and outcome of each interview in the employer contact files. Finally, have students send thank you notes to all employers who interview them. Students should learn how to follow-up a job interview with a short note. This contact is their opportunity to thank the employer, emphasize to the employer how interested they are in the position, and provide any additional information requested in the interview. A sample student thank you letter is included in Appendix 3.10.

Follow up with employers to finalize job placements

Check back with all employers who provided interviews. If an employer doesn't contact the student within a reasonable period of time after the interview, have the student check to determine the status of the job opening. Program staff may also want to ask the employer for feedback on the student's performance during the interview, and their perception of the student's potential for success on the job. This insight enables staff to better prepare students for future interviews and job opportunities.

Before the student makes a final decision on a job placement, discuss the pros and cons of the job with the student, and with the vocational rehabilitation (VR) counselor if this student is a VR client, and decide if this job placement fits the abilities and interests of the student. Consider the following issues in this discussion:

- Is the student interested in this type of work? Does the job fit the student's projected career goals?

- Does the student have the basic skills needed to be successful on the job? Will the job need to be modified for this student?

- Where is the job located? Is it within walking distance or near public transportation?

- What are the wages and working hours? Does the job provide benefits, further training, or other aspects that would promote upward mobility?

Once the student has a firm job offer from an employer, there are a few final details to be worked out before the first day on the job. The student and employer should schedule a date for the student to start on-the-job training. They should also agree on a weekly schedule for the student. Be sure to help the student plan transportation arrangements (e.g. walking, driving, bus, etc.) and provide transportation training if needed. Finally, the student should find out if any special equipment or clothing will be needed for the job, and make arrangements to purchase these before the job begins.

Provide Job Training and Support

Plan and prepare for job placement

At this point, an initial determination was made by program staff and the student that a reasonably good match existed between the student's skills and abilities and the expectations and requirements of the position. Now is the time to translate this initial decision into a more systematic training plan. Whenever possible, you should visit the job site prior to the student's first day of work to identify: (a) the specific job duties associated with the position; (b) any special tools, clothing, or equipment that may be needed and not supplied by the employer; (c) any job accommodations or training strategies that might be needed to assist the student in performing the job, and (d) whether job training will be provided by the employer/job supervisor, a program staff member, or both. A sample Job Duties Checklist is included in Appendix 3.11.

This on-site support service will be resisted by some employers and welcomed by others. This is true for students as well; some students do not want any on-site support from program staff if it gives the appearance they are somehow different from other employees. It is critical that program staff be sensitive to these concerns by employers and students. Staff should negotiate strategies in advance to provide a level of training support that is both acceptable and appropriate and that will maximize the student's independence, integration, and success on the job.

Next, all parties should sign a written training agreement. A training agreement is designed to document the roles and responsibilities of all the people involved in the job training process, including the student, employer, school staff, parent(s), and VR counselor if this student is a VR client. Written agreements also can be helpful in meeting Department of Labor standards for unpaid job placements. Set up a meeting with all relevant participants to discuss the purposes of the job placement and the roles and responsibilities of each person who will be signing the agreement. When everyone understands their respective responsibilities, sign the training agreement and give copies to all parties. A sample written training agreement is included in Appendix 3.12.

Provide on-the-job training

On the first day of the job, a program staff member and/or the job supervisor should explain the general job duties and the expectations of the employer to the student. This is also the time for the student to complete any paperwork required by the employer. Actual training begins after the orientation is completed. Training can be conducted by the employer, the program staff member, or both. Ideally, this decision was made prior to the student's first day of work. In deciding who should provide the initial training, consider the following factors:

- How complicated are the job duties? How much experience does the program staff member have with the job tasks? For example, one student in a YTP site was placed with a metal fabrication company installing heating ducts. The staff member had no experience in this area. Therefore, the primary training was provided by the job-site supervisor. The staff member was available to provide support to the student and job supervisor as needed.

- Is the time that the employer/job-site supervisor has available for training sufficient to meet the student's needs? Are there any special training or job accommodation considerations? If either of these issues are present, is there an appropriate role that program staff can play to supplement this training? Or, are there individuals at the job site who can provide support to the student? Support may be provided by co-workers who take an interest in the success of the new worker and mentor that new worker toward independence.

Whether working alone or with an employer, you should follow a systematic process to teach the job duties. Remember that students—like all people—learn differently. Some students will learn quite well through oral directions, others need visual/graphical guidance, and others learn best by performing the task. Using all of these teaching modes will increase the likelihood that students will understand and remember what they're being taught. Also remember that many employers/job-site supervisors are so familiar with the job duties they are teaching that they often forget what it is like to learn this job for the first time. This might mean that critical aspects of job performance could be overlooked during the instruction process. If the employer/job-site supervisor is taking major responsibility for the training, take note of areas where you believe the student may require further training support.

Build self-monitoring strategies into the training process from the very beginning. It is critical for students to develop skills at monitoring and evaluating their own job performance. Explain to students that self-monitoring is a method for watching and checking themselves to insure that the job is done right. Self-monitoring strategies can be useful for several aspects of job performance. For example, a checklist of daily tasks could be created, allowing students to monitor and check off each task as it is completed. Similarly, students could identify other work behaviors they want to improve (e.g., arrive on time to work, or get along with the supervisor), write these goals down, and then rate their performance at the end of each day. Self-monitoring devices can take virtually any form and size; they can include checklists, graphical organizers, or any other tool that communicates the essential information to the student, and they can range in size from a standard sheet of notebook paper carried on a clipboard to a laminated card carried in a shirt pocket. Students should assume major responsibility for designing the self-monitoring strategy they will be using as it must be something that works for them on the job. Program staff often will need to help students: (a) identify relevant job behaviors, (b) design and construct a self-monitoring strategy, and (c) learn how to use their strategy effectively to monitor and evaluate their performance. Examples of self-monitoring tools created by students and staff in several local YTP sites are included in Appendix 3.13.

Develop a monitoring schedule and provide follow-along support as needed

You will want to move into a monitoring phase as soon as the student can perform the job independently. Your monitoring should begin with a fairly frequent schedule of visits (e.g., every other day or twice a week), with the frequency of site visits being reduced (e.g., once per week, once every two weeks, once per month) as students settle into a comfortable routine on the job. Discuss your monitoring schedule, and the reasons behind your decisions, with both the employer and the student. Both should feel comfortable with this monitoring process, and both should be aware that you will continue to be available: (a) to answer questions, (b) assist in resolving any problems that arise, and (c) obtain regular feedback about how the placement is going.

Even if a student is working completely independently, it is still important to check in with the employer at least monthly. By checking with an employer, you can deal with any difficulties the student may be having on the job *before* they escalate. It is better to call an employer and find out everything is going fine than to have an employer call because things are so bad that the student is about to be fired. You should work with the student and the employer to solve any problems that arise with the student's job performance.

Document your visits to the job site and the phone calls or other formal contacts you have with the employer. Any problems the student is having on the job and the interventions provided by staff should be also be noted. This documentation can occur on a simple Case Note Form (Appendix 3.14). In addition, approximately once per month you should obtain a formal rating of the student's performance from the employer. A sample Monthly Progress Report is included in Appendix 3.15. Place this documentation in the student's file to provide an ongoing progress record. Regularly scheduled employer evaluations give the employer a format to communicate the problems and success the student is having on the job. Documentation provides a record of the student's progress, accomplishments, and continuing needs, which allows the student, employer, and program staff to base discussions about performance on specific instances of relevance to the student rather than abstract principles about "good employees." Often these issues can become topics of discussion in Job Club (see Chapter 2), and the focus of specific goal-setting activities with students.

Finally, throughout all these activities, look for opportunities to build support systems on the job site. These support networks have the potential to supplement and continue the training and follow-along support provided by program staff. This process moves the support from an artificial source (i.e., program staff) to one that is more typical to most employment circumstances. Most employees obtain some degree of support and training from co-workers. You may have to initiate students in how to access this support network. At the same time, the employer and co-workers may have to learn how to make that support network more available by designating mentors or lead workers that take over the function of program staff as they reduce their level and intensity of follow-along support.

CREATING ADDITIONAL PROGRAM OPTIONS TO BUILD STUDENT WORK SKILLS

The preceding sections of this chapter described procedures for creating employment options for students with individual employers in the community. As mentioned at the beginning of the chapter, this more traditional job development approach will most likely be your bottom line strategy for job placement. There are, however, a number of other approaches that create employment options for students. This section of the chapter describes three additional strategies for creating employment options for students: (a) school–business partnerships, (b) school-based enterprises, and (c) student-employee leasing programs. These approaches are summarized in Table 3.1.

Although your ultimate employment goal is placement in paid jobs, there are many paths up the mountain. Taking a wider view of the employment process beyond employer recruitment, job placement, and job training and support offers several advantages for a comprehensive school-to-work program. First, it creates a new range of opportunities for your students to learn about the world of work. All of the program strategies described here build a work-related foundation for adolescents and young adults while creating relationships with the business community. Job development with individual employers can be frustrating if your students have little or no understanding of the business community or the world of work. The programs described in this section will provide additional opportunities to help students build solid work skills. In addition, this view also sets the stage for *building long-term collaborative school-to-work programs* as business and education learn to work together to develop a more prepared and competitive workforce.

These approaches were developed by local YTP sites to meet the unique needs of their students and community. As part of your planning process, you should consider the unique characteristics of your local site as well so you develop a model that will fit the needs of your students, school, and community. For example, your community may support a diverse manufacturing base. In addition to actual employment, there might be an opportunity through a school–business partnership to develop on-site classes in a local

Table 3.1
Summary of Employment Program Options

Feature	School–Business Partnerships	School-Based Enterprises	Student–Employee Leasing Programs
Program Overview	Partnerships linking businesses with specific schools or programs within a school.	Small businesses developed and operated by students and school staff.	School districts become a temporary services agency and lease student–employees to local businesses.
Business Commitment	Time commitment from individual business person, and/or financial commitment to provide resources to school.	No direct business commitment. Businesses might employ students trained by the school.	Businesses hire students through a contract with the school district. Requires time commitment to develop initial contract, and supervise student employees.
School Commitment	Staff time to develop partnership, and participate in partnership activities.	Staff time to conduct market survey, and develop and operate the business. Initial financial investment (typically ranging from $250 to over $5,000) to purchase equipment and supplies.	Staff time to develop contracts with businesses and monitor student progress. Administrative support from school district to provide bookkeeping and payroll services.
Unique Benefits to Students and Sites	Provides students with realistic picture of the world of work. Develops long-term relationships between school and business.	Provides students with opportunities to learn how to manage a business. Generates income to support school-to-work or other programs.	Provides students with hands-on training in a structured environment. Generates income to support school-to-work or other school programs.

manufacturer's business to expose students to that potential occupation. On the other hand, you may not have a strong local economy, but you have a core group of motivated students that could easily create a small business venture. Or, your employment community may be interested in contracting with your program or school district to establish a stable source of temporary workers that come with some support systems, similar to the student–employee leasing model. Attending to these needs in the planning process will increase your rate of success and reduce the likelihood that you will experience the consternation Calvin is experiencing in the following cartoon.

Calvin and Hobbes
by Bill Watterson

School–Business Partnerships

There are many different types of school–business partnerships, ranging from simple sponsorship activities (e.g., school teams, recognition programs, etc.) to complex collaboration efforts (e.g., Business/Education Compacts, City Alliances, Youth Investment Projects, etc.). All school–business partnerships require a commitment from a local business (either time or money or both), and a commitment from school staff (usually time to develop and manage partnership activities). Examples of partnership activities are included in Table 3.2.

Partnership activities benefit students by providing an initial connection to the real world of work. Employers benefit from a better understanding of the school system, and a better prepared workforce. The experiences of one YTP site with creating and using a school–business partnership to

Table 3.2
Sample Partnership Activities

Businesses can provide:	Schools can provide:
✔ Career interest activities ✔ Mentors or tutors for individual students ✔ Field trips of the work place ✔ Job-shadowing opportunities ✔ Speakers for classrooms ✔ Recognition for student achievement ✔ Job experience or training	✔ Students who are trained for a specific job ✔ Support for students placed on site ✔ Use of school facilities ✔ Positive publicity for the business

address the work-based learning needs of students are described in the following vignette.

. . . .

Beaver City School–Business Partnership

The entire school-to-work team was excited when they heard that Janette had finally found a paid community job. After several years of intensive vocational training and assistance with independent living skills, Janette was ready to transition into independent employment. The only problem now was transportation. Janette's disability prevented her from obtaining a driver's license. Her mother also had a disability and could not be relied upon for transportation assistance. Public transportation was Janette's only real option. But Janette's mother was very protective, and she was unwilling to allow her to travel alone in the city.

Despite these obstacles, the school-to-work coordinator refused to give up on the dream of helping Janette work independently in the community. He decided to ask the mother if she would allow her daughter to travel independently if she had a reliable means of communication (i.e., Janette could call Mom, Mom could call her, Janette could access 911 in an emergency). With the support of the mother, the teacher approached a local phone company to see if they would be interested in donating some cellular technology to help support a student in transition from school-to-work. The company was very interested, and, in fact, was already considering doing some research on the efficacy of using cellular telephones by individuals with disabilities. The cellular executives had also hoped to develop a "special needs rate plan" that would make the technology affordable for individuals who are financially stretched. A few weeks later, Janette was outfitted with a small phone that she kept in a fanny pack, an earpiece, and a small microphone. Riding back and forth to work on the city bus, she had the assurance of having phone access but looked like any other teenager "listening to tunes" on a radio.

What started as an agreement to meet the needs of one student quickly evolved into a formal school–business partnership. As part of the agreement, the school district now receives loaned equipment and donated air time to use with both staff and students. The cellular company receives field test data from students, as well as potential long-term customers. In addition, the company receives public recognition for their active involvement in supporting students in transition and as a leader in telecommunications access for individuals with disabilities. The partner-

ship agreement has been expanded to include occupational exploration opportunities for students and opportunities for teacher internships
in the cellular industry.

. . . .

To develop a school–business partnership, begin by gathering information that will help you develop your specific concepts. Talk with other
school districts in your community, region, or state that have developed
partnerships to gather information on how they have set up their particular
partnerships. Call your state Department of Education to obtain the names
of school districts that have developed partnerships if you are not aware of
any in your area. Using this information, develop a brief program description that outlines the general structure of the partnership, including goals
and the students it is intended to serve. Even though this overview will
change as you refine your plan, it will be helpful to have your preliminary
ideas in writing as you gather support for developing a school–business partnership between your program and the business community. Based on our
experiences with local sites that participate in the YTP, we recommend
seven steps to develop an effective school–business partnership:

1. obtain support for your concept within the school;
2. obtain support within the community;
3. select an appropriate business partner;
4. develop the materials that will be needed for the partnership;
5. select the students who will be involved in the partnership;
6. implement partnership activities; and
7. monitor and evaluate its success on an ongoing basis.

Obtain support within the school

Before you can implement a school–business partnership you need to have
school administrative support. Obtaining administrative buy-in and input
will afford you a higher probability of success and continuation as you go
about creating innovative opportunities for students to explore the world of
work through partnerships. Consider setting up a meeting (or a series of meetings) with school administrators to discuss your plans for a school–business
partnership. Specific issues to discuss include:

Developing the partnership concept

- What are the goals of the partnership?
- What format should the partnership take?
- How will the partnership benefit the school in general as well as the individual students?
- How will the partnership benefit the participating business?
- How will the partnership be coordinated with other existing school-to-work transition activities?

Partnership activities

- Who will be responsible for connecting with local businesses to develop partnerships?
- What specific activities will be offered to students?
- Which students will be selected to participate?
- How will partnership activities be worked into the existing school schedule?

Monitoring and evaluating the partnership

- Who will serve as liaison between the school and participating business?
- Who will schedule students and monitor student participation?
- How will the effectiveness of the partnership be evaluated?

Remember that other programs within the school, such as professional–technical education programs or cooperative work experience programs, may have relationships with business partners within the community. It is important to be aware of these existing relationships and understand how your new program fits into the bigger picture of school-to-work transition activities for all students. There is nothing worse than having businesses close their doors to partnerships with the school because they have become overwhelmed by a variety of vocational and transition programs clamoring for their participation.

Obtain support within the community

Identify community members who show interest in partnerships or who might be instrumental in connecting you to the business community, such as members of the Chamber of Commerce. Look also toward local employers who have prior positive relationships with school programs, and the pool of employers who have worked previously with your program. Be creative and consider the range of possibilities that might attract a business to consider a formal partnership with your program. Some business leaders are very concerned about the broader issues of preparation of the future workforce and influencing education, while others may be more interested in being involved as work experience or employment sites only. Use your networking know-how to find and locate these potential partners and begin to develop a list of possibilities.

Select an appropriate business partner

Assuming you have been able to work as a team with your school administration to identify the specific goals of your program and have identified a list of potential business partners, the next step is to target a specific business to help you develop your partnership activities. Selection may be driven by a number of factors, including: (a) the reputation of a specific business as a strong supporter of educational issues, (b) the marketing and public relations needs of the business, and/or (c) the fact that someone in your program knows that "Cathy Smith, the CEO of Wooster Widgets, is a real champion for at-risk students and would love to get involved with our program as a partner."

Develop materials needed for the partnership

There are a great variety of materials that could be developed to support your school–business partnership (e.g., brochures, procedures manuals, evaluation forms, multimedia presentations, etc.), and eventually you may want to develop all of these to support and describe your program. One of the first documents you will want to develop, however, is a written agreement between your program/school and each of your participating business partners. Written agreements greatly reduce the possibility of misunderstanding between partners regarding the purpose and specifics of the partnership. A sample agreement is included in Appendix 3.16.

As you identify and develop the specific materials to support your program, don't reinvent the wheel. School districts that have developed school–business partnerships often have forms and procedures manuals related to their partnership activities, and they are usually willing to share or sell these to interested parties. Similarly, many schools and businesses will have materials you could adapt for your school–business partnership. For example, cooperative work experience programs may have written agreement forms that could be adapted to create a written school–business partnership agreement. Some businesses may have training feedback or marketing surveys that could assist you in evaluating the effectiveness of the partnership. Volunteer programs in the schools often have materials and procedures that may dovetail nicely with minor adaptations to a school–business partnership. Examine all of these possibilities and decide whether you want to adapt materials that have already been developed or develop your own materials to meet the needs of your particular circumstances.

Select students to be involved in the partnership

Collaborate with your business partner to select students to participate in the program. Specific decisions regarding student selection and level of participation should be based on the details of the partnership and the interests of students. For example, a partnership may include having supervisors come to the school to talk with students about job interviewing strategies and may allow students opportunities to go to the company to conduct informational interviews with workers who are performing a high-technology manufacturing job. It may not make sense for students who have not expressed interest in this occupation to participate in the visit to the manufacturing site. However, it is conceivable that all students would benefit from participating in the class discussions on job interviewing strategies. It is also a good idea to make these activities available to other students enrolled in vocational education or professional–technical programs. Students with special needs will benefit from participating in an integrated program, and you will also promote the concept that your program is just one component of a larger school-to-work strategy for all students.

Participate in partnership activities

The adage *quality rather than quantity* applies well in this phase of your partnership. Build your program from activities that can be implemented easily and successfully. Although you already may have developed some ideas for activities during the initial phases of planning for your partnership, you now need to obtain the input and support of your business partner. Partnership activities should be interesting, fun, and beneficial to students and employers. Remember that some activities may unfold over the school year, such as a series of job shadowing visits for various students, and some may focus on a single event, such as a career fair. As your partnership develops, you may agree to participate in more involved activities, such as student apprenticeship programs or teacher internships in industry. Remain flexible so that both partners can adapt and redesign activities as needed.

Evaluate partnership success on an ongoing basis

The final step in developing any new program is to evaluate its impact. Decide on a monitoring and evaluation form, and participate with your business partner in determining the overall effectiveness of the relationship. You should evaluate the partnership in terms of the impact on the business as well as its impact on the schools. Students who participate in the partnership should also have the opportunity to evaluate their experiences. Based on this feedback, the partners can decide if the program needs to be revised.

School-based Enterprises

School-based businesses are identified consistently in the school-to-work literature as an essential component of a comprehensive school-to-work program. And for good reason. School-based enterprises can: (a) be established in virtually any community, rural and nonrural; (b) be any type of business imaginable as long as it provides a legal, valuable service to the school and/or community; (c) generate income to support student and staff wages, and profits to support other aspects of your school-to-work program; (d) teach valuable work and business skills to students; and (e) provide opportunities to develop integrated school-to-work programs for students with and without special needs. YTP sites in Oregon that have developed school-based enterprises have experienced all of these advantages. The experiences of one YTP site with creating and using a school-based enterprise to address the work-based learning needs of students are described in the following vignette.

. . . .

River Valley School-based Enterprise

It's springtime in Oregon, and a group of young people are enjoying a beautiful day in the mountains. But this is not your ordinary nature hike—these teens are carefully staking and marking local wildflowers so they can collect the seeds later in the year. They call themselves the Wild Bunch Seed Company, and for them the profits are far greater than the money brought in for seeds marketed under their label. As they learn various phases of the business, they also have a chance to practice academic and business skills. "It's a chance to do something other than schoolwork, but stay involved with school," comments one of the students. In this business, "you are really learning about the environment and you earn a little extra money."

A joint project of the staff and students, the idea for a seed catalog company sprouted from a discussion between two teachers who had an interest in local plants and a commitment to alternative education. Their idea was to bring a money making venture into the classroom to give the students an opportunity to apply skills they were learning in academic classes. The business started with an initial investment of $150 to purchase seeds and envelopes. Later, school staff received a small grant from a regional private foundation to purchase a seed cleaner along with some additional equipment and supplies.

In the first year of the project, the students packaged and sold seeds purchased wholesale from Oregon growers. All of the seeds were test-grown locally, and only the most successful were selected for mail order sales. In this phase, students were responsible for creating and publishing a catalog and distributing it door-to-door. They also learned to keep inventory and take the orders that came in from as far away as Arizona and California. During the second phase of the business, students went out into the field to collect and identify seeds not usually offered commercially. This phase provided an opportunity for students to learn science (conservation, ecology, botany) and social studies (local geography, community preservation, etc.) in addition to the math, accounting, and marketing skills learned in the earlier phases. Students participating in the business also consulted with local plant experts through the Native Plant Society.

The Wild Bunch Seed Company currently operates in the fall and spring, generating $2,000 to $3,000 per school year. About half the revenue goes back to support the business; the remainder is divided among students based on the hours each has worked. But this business is not just about profits. One of the teachers described the transformation in his at-risk students, saying , "These students are really motivated to work. They find out why it is necessary to learn math as they help with books, add up orders, and measure and weigh seeds. They learn language skills as they market their seeds to the community. All of your basic subjects are brought to life in this project."

. . . .

As attractive as these advantages are it is very hard work to develop a business that is equally successful at providing students with training opportunities and generating profits for your program. You should approach the development of a school-based enterprise carefully and systematically, just as anyone should who is aspiring to develop a profitable small business in the community. If you are interested in developing a school-based business, begin by gathering information that will help you develop your ideas. Talk with other school districts in your community, region, or state that have developed school-based enterprises. Call your state Department of Education to obtain the names of school districts that have developed school-based businesses if you are not aware of any in your area. In addition, a potentially valuable resource for advice can be found through the Small Business Administration office in your area. They have a group of retired executives (Service Corps of Retired Executives) who provide free consultation to individuals who are developing small businesses. Another resource might be found through your local community college, which may offer classes for individuals interested in starting their own businesses. Based on our experiences with local YTP sites in Oregon, we recommend eight steps to develop an effective school-based enterprise:

1. survey the community and develop a preliminary business plan;

2. obtain support for your concept within the school;

3. select students to participate in the business;

4. develop the materials needed to run a successful small business;

5. purchase equipment and supplies;

6. advertise your product;

7. staff and run the business; and

8. evaluate the success of the business.

Survey the community and develop a preliminary business plan

Although local employers will not be directly involved in operating your business, *it is important to be sensitive to the local community as you move ahead with your plan*. You should survey the community to determine if there is a market for your product. For example, if you are planning to develop an Espresso business and there are already coffee carts on every other block in town, there probably isn't a need for another one, even if its profits go to support local schools. Think about how your business will impact, or possibly compete with, other small employers in the community. While there may always be some element of competition between the business you develop and other similar businesses in the community, you should be sensitive to the potential public relations issues that could emerge if the school is viewed as an "unfair competitor" by members of the community. Finally, consider the type of training students will receive by participating in your business. Will any of these skills be transferable to community employers? Will the skills students acquire be considered a benefit by the school and community employers? The answers to these questions will help you decide what type of business will be most appropriate and most successful in your community. Think creatively and entrepreneurially in this process. The possibilities for new businesses are virtually endless. Examples of several school-based enterprises developed by YTP sites in Oregon are included in Table 3.3.

Using the information gathered from your community survey, develop a tentative business plan. Consider using the services of a consultant from the Service Corps of Retired Executives to help you develop this plan, and address the following questions:

- What product or service will you sell?
- Who are your potential customers?
- What kind of advertising or marketing strategies do you need?
- What occupational skills are associated with the business that could be beneficial for students and community employers?
- How will you staff and run the business?
- What are the initial and ongoing costs of operating the business?

Obtain support within the school

Before you initiate a small business, you need to have school administrative support. Set up a meeting (or more likely a series of meetings) with school administrators, including the person with risk management responsibilities, to obtain their input and support for developing the business. Specific issues to be discussed include:

Developing the business

- Does the school district have any policies regarding school-based enterprises?

Table 3.3
Sample School-based Enterprises Developed by YTP Sites in Oregon

Name of Business	Product or Service	Student Participation *Students in this business are responsible for:*	Start-up Costs Materials Needed	Student Scheduling	Focus of Instruction
Apple Cart Espresso Bar	coffee drinks baked goods	✓ preparing specialty drinks ✓ maintaining product inventory ✓ selling products to customers	$5,000 for purchasing espresso cart, cups, coffee, flavored syrups, paper products, & other food supplies	2-hour blocks 5 days per week	Students complete 6-10 week training program in: ✓ money handling ✓ communication ✓ customer service
Comets Classic Carry-out	take-out meals	✓ planning menus ✓ shopping for groceries ✓ preparing & packaging meals	$300 for kitchen equipment & food supplies	1 class period per day	Students receive individual and group instruction in: ✓ accounting ✓ comparison shopping ✓ nutrition/meal planning ✓ safety/hygiene
WildBunch Seed Company	wholesale & mail order seed packets	✓ collecting & identifying wildflower seeds ✓ packaging seeds ✓ developing catalogs ✓ developing marketing materials	$150 for seeds & envelopes	90-minute block 2 or 3 days per week	Students receive career education and work experience credit for completing assignments in ✓ horticulture ✓ consumer math ✓ business accounting
Winter Garden	organic produce	✓ planning garden layouts & preparing soil ✓ building greenhouses ✓ harvesting & packaging ✓ marketing produce to local restaurants & markets	$850 for seeds, garden tools, and materials for greenhouse	twice a week after school	Students complete curriculum assignments in: ✓ organic gardening ✓ business/marketing

- What liability and licensure issues need to be addressed?

- How much are initial start up costs, and how will these expenses be met?

- How will profits, if any, be processed through the school's business office?

- Who will be responsible for developing and managing the business?

- How will this business coordinate activities with other school-to-work transition activities?

Student participation

- Which students will participate in the business, and what will their responsibilities be?

- How will student participation affect daily school schedules?

- Will students receive credit for participation?

- Will students be paid wages?

Monitoring and evaluating the business

- What skills will be taught and how will student progress be measured and evaluated?

- How will the overall program be evaluated?

Remember that other programs within the school, such as professional–technical education programs or cooperative work experience programs, may have small business ventures within the school or community. It is important to be aware of these existing school-based enterprises, and understand how your new program fits into the bigger picture of school-to-work transition activities for all students. Also remember that it is a lengthy and sometimes frustrating process to work within the existing bureaucracy of a school system to create a for-profit venture. You will need to remain focused and patient as you proceed.

Select students to participate

Student participation will be influenced by existing class and work schedules. As part of the selection process, explain the goals of the business to students and get an initial commitment from them to participate. Provide opportunities for students to be involved in the management decisions of the business as much as possible so they can experience the entire process of developing and operating a business. Also, consider involving other vocational education or business students in your venture. These students may be interested in helping you with the day-to-day tasks of operating the business or they may want to be involved only in specific projects such as developing a marketing strategy.

Develop the materials needed to run a successful small business

Any small business requires a certain amount of paperwork to run smoothly. In addition, because you are developing a school-to-work *training* program, you will need to develop materials that will structure and support these training activities. Consider the skill levels of your students and the needs of your specific business as you develop (or adapt) these materials. Some of the materials you may need include:

Training materials

- Job descriptions for each position in the business
- Training outlines, including task analyses for certain components of the business (for example, list of steps in making a mocha espresso)
- Training certificates
- Information matching curriculum goals to skills taught in the business

Advertising or marketing information

- Brochures
- Catalogs listing products, and prices
- Flyers advertising the business

Accounting and inventory procedures

- Order forms
- Inventory sheets
- Time sheets
- Procedures for payroll

Purchase equipment and supplies

Most new businesses require an initial financial investment. Depending on your business, your costs may include purchasing specific equipment (such as an espresso machine) or materials and supplies (such as flavored coffees, milk, and paper cups). It is always a good idea to start small and build your inventory later when you know what your profit margin will be. Start-up costs for the small businesses described in this chapter range from $150 for the seed company to $5,000 for the espresso cart business.

Advertise your product

It is important to get the word out about your product, even if your business is school-based and geared toward student customers. Develop flyers or catalogs to provide information to your potential customers. You may want to prepare some special promotional materials for the "grand opening" of your new business.

Provide training to students as needed

Before you serve your first customer you will need to provide some hands-on training to teach students specific tasks required to operate a business, such as making change or taking and shipping orders. Some school districts have worked with local employers to develop curriculum packages geared to the demands of a specific industry. The type and amount of training you provide will depend on the skill level of your students and the needs of your business. Once the training is completed, develop a daily schedule for students and staff who will be operating the business.

Staff and run the business

When you have finished purchasing all your supplies, and preparing all of your paperwork, you can finally get down to opening your business! This is the time when all your preparation finally pays off and you can begin to sell your product or service. One of the major challenges in running school-based enterprises is having enough staff to supervise operations on a daily basis. This has proven to be especially difficult when the business operates during evening or weekend hours. Some school sites have hired additional staff who take over the primary responsibility of supervising students and managing business decisions such as product inventory and bookkeeping. Other sites have given some of these responsibilities to student managers. Although one of your goals is to make a profit, remember that the motivation of your business is to help your students learn valuable skills. Be flexible enough to allow your students to make important business decisions and experience the impact of these decisions. These real-world experiences will truly help prepare students for the transition into community employment.

Evaluate the success of the business

The final step in developing any new program is to evaluate its impact. Creating a small business from scratch is not easy, so allow yourself a grace period before evaluating your success too harshly. When you are ready, program staff can collect information from customers as well as students to measure the success of the venture. Although you certainly will want to consider the profits as one marker of success, your yardstick to measure success should be the intangible benefits that students receive from participating in the development and operation of a brand new business. Staff and students should discuss the need to modify business operating procedures and ultimately decide if it is feasible (and profitable) to continue operations.

Student–Employee Leasing Programs

One of the more unique components of a comprehensive school-to-work program could well be the concept of student–employee leasing programs. This concept, quite similar to the temporary employment services provided by private sector agencies, offers several advantages. First, it fulfills a pressing need for workers in many rural and nonrural communities. Many community employers are frustrated with the lack of trained workers and with the headaches of screening, hiring, and firing employees. A school-sponsored student–employee leasing program can provide employers with well-trained, pre-screened student-employees at a reasonable rate. Second, it can provide students with a variety of paid work experiences in the community. Finally, it has the potential to generate income to support student and staff salaries and profits to support other aspects of your school-to-work program. The experiences of one YTP site with creating and using a student–employee leasing program to address the work-based learning needs of students are described in the following vignette.

. . . .

Emerald Student-Employee Leasing Program

The bright pink flyer on the bulletin board read "Welcome to the BEST program! BEST (Business Education Site Training) is an exciting new venture of the Emerald School District to provide employee leasing services to area businesses. It allows students to *earn* while they *learn* a job. The district makes money too!" This simple flyer was the result of six months of intensive work by several teachers, key administrators, and staff from the school district personnel and business offices who worked in collaboration with a business advisory board to create this new school-to-work option.

The BEST employee leasing program was developed to respond to two related but different needs. School-to-work staff wanted to develop more community-based training opportunities for students in transition. The staff wanted to help students obtain paid positions, yet still felt the need to offer structured training to build competitive work skills. At the same time, many local employers were concerned about the quality of the entry-level workforce. Most of their new hires from the school district or the community at large simply did not have the basic skills needed to meet competitive standards. A lot of money was spent screening, hiring, and training these young workers, who often did not stay with the job long enough to warrant the initial investment.

To answer both of these needs, the school district took on the commitment of functioning as a temporary employment agency, providing a trained workforce to local employers. The district personnel department was responsible for screening and hiring the student employees, negotiating fair contracts with local employers, and processing the monthly payroll checks. School-to-work staff made the initial connections with community employers and provided on-site training and monitoring to student workers. During the first year of the BEST program, students filled temporary positions in a variety of businesses, including a large hotel/conference center, a nursing home, a metal stamping plant, and a carpet installation company. After 2 to 4 months the students were either hired as permanent employees or moved into other paid training positions in a different occupation.

This program has been a big success for the school district and the participating employers. Employers have the benefit of a pre-screened and trained workforce, while students learn work skills and earn wages. In the words of one school administrator, "employee leasing creates a win-win partnership for schools and businesses."

. . . .

You should approach the development of a student–employee leasing program in the same careful and systematic manner that you would approach the development of a school-based business, because that is after all exactly what you are doing—developing a business. Begin by gathering information and advice. A potential source of information are temporary service agencies in your community. These agencies may be able to provide you with some basic operating information about their business, and a sense of the competition in your community for this type of service. You may also want to contact the Small Business Agency in your area—and the Service Corps of Retired Executives that they administer—to determine whether they have any consultants with experience in operating employment agencies. Based on our experiences with local sites that participate in the YTP, we recommend eight steps to develop an effective student–employee leasing program:

1. survey the community and develop a preliminary business plan;

2. obtain support for your concept within the school;

3. develop the materials needed to operate a successful employee leasing program;

4. identify potential business partners and negotiate contracts with specific employers;

5. select students to participate;

6. place students on site with employers;

7. provide follow-up support to students and employers; and

8. evaluate the success of the business.

Survey the employers in your community and develop a preliminary plan

Employers are critical partners in successful employee leasing programs. Through negotiated contracts with the school district, in essence they hire the school district to provide student employees for their business. Before developing an employee leasing program at your site, *you need to be sure that employers in your community would be interested and willing to support such a program.* Talk to some of the employers you already know through your employment network and find out whether they would be interested in purchasing this type of service from the school district.

Once you have completed this survey, review the information you have gathered and develop a preliminary plan for establishing a student–employee leasing program in your district. This plan should include, at minimum, a brief overview of your employee leasing program, the need for the program in the community, goals, and the benefits to employers, students, and the school district. This written overview will be a helpful lobbying tool to win support for the program within the school district.

Obtain support within the school

Even more than developing a small business, creating a district-sponsored employee leasing program requires extensive support from the school administration. As you are discussing this idea and beginning to formulate your plans, establish a working relationship with key people in the following departments within your school district: (a) personnel, (b) payroll, (c) business/fiscal services, and (d) risk management. Schedule a series of meetings with these key school administrators to obtain their input and support for developing the program. Specific issues to be discussed include:

Developing the employee leasing program

- Does the school district have any policies or procedures regarding the hiring of temporary employees (students or adults)?
- What liability and contractual issues need to be addressed?
- Who will market the program and negotiate contracts with local employers?
- Who will have ultimate responsibility for hiring and firing student employees?
- How will payroll be processed through the school's business office?
- How will profits be processed through the school's business office?
- How will this program coordinate activities with other school-to-work transition activities?

Student participation

- Which students will participate in the program, and what will their responsibilities be?
- How will student participation affect daily school schedules?
- Will students receive credit for participation?

Monitoring and evaluating the program

- What skills will be taught, and how will student progress be measured and evaluated?

- How will the overall program be evaluated?

These issues will not be resolved overnight. This could be a new and challenging venture for many school districts. For those YTP sites that have managed to work through the complicated start-up process, the rewards have been substantial. Student–employee leasing programs provide paid training to students, and they generate income for the school-to-work programs within the school district.

Develop the materials needed to operate a student–employee leasing program

An employee leasing program requires a certain amount of paperwork to run smoothly. Some of the materials you may need to develop include:

Advertising and marketing materials

- Materials describing the employee leasing program, including benefits to employers and students

- Flyers or brochures advertising the program

Administrative and payroll procedures

- Employment policies

- Sample contracts between schools and employers

- Time sheets

- Procedures for payroll

Identify potential business partners and negotiate contracts with specific employers

It is probably wise to start small, developing your employee leasing program with a limited number of students and only one or two employers. You may want to recruit employers with whom you have already established relationships, such as employers who have hired your students in the past. Also, give priority to larger employers who could conceivably hire more than one student and offer more than one type of job training at their location. YTP sites that have developed employee leasing programs have placed student–employees with a variety of businesses, including carpet companies, nursing homes, metal manufacturing and stamping plants, motels, and food service operations.

You will want to develop a specific written contract with each participating employer. The contract should specify the amount per hour that the school district will charge for each employee, and the specific services your program staff will provide the employer. A sample contract is included in Appendix 3.17. The contract should be fair to the employer, and also provide enough profit to the district to sustain the program. Successful employee leasing programs have found they need to charge $6 to $8 per hour per student in order to pay the student employees minimum wage and generate enough profits to support the program.

Select students to participate

You should recruit a sufficient pool of students to adequately fulfill any contracts you have negotiated. Although you may be developing this program primarily to meet the needs of your students with special needs, it is a good idea to open it up to other students enrolled in vocational education or professional–technical programs. By including students with a range of abilities and skills, you can provide employees to fill a variety of positions. For example, in a metal fabrication plant, some students may be packaging parts and filling orders, while others with more advanced skills may serve as apprentice tool and die makers. As part of the selection process, provide an opportunity for students to tour the business and understand the demands of the worksite.

Place students on site with employers

In a typical employee leasing program, school districts provide all of the initial screening and hiring of the student employees. Technically, the students are employed by the school district even though they are working in a community business. School district staff then have the responsibility for matching student employees with appropriate employers. Many employers want to be involved in this matching process, and will schedule an interview as if the business were screening potential job candidates. After the interview process, staff should work cooperatively with the employer to develop a regular work schedule and provide any initial on-site training needed.

Provide follow-up support to students and employers

Another critical component of an employee leasing program is the support and training provided to students on the job. This is a short-term training opportunity for students, and staff need to ensure that students learn the general work behaviors as well as specific work skills needed to succeed on the job. At the conclusion of their training (anywhere from 2 to 4 months), students may be hired as permanent employees of the business, or they may move on to another community training site. During the training process, program staff also need to work closely with the employers to address any training or administrative concerns that may arise.

Evaluate the success of the program

The final step in developing any new program is to evaluate its impact. An employee leasing program is a major project, so allow a grace period to work the kinks out of the program before you evaluate it too harshly. Program staff should collect information from employers as well as students to measure the success of this program. Although you certainly will want to consider the profits as one marker of success, keep in mind that the motivation of your project is the intangible benefits students receive from learning skills in a real world setting. Staff should discuss the need to modify the program, and ultimately decide if it is feasible to continue operations.

APPENDIX 3.1
STEPS FOR CREATING AN EMPLOYER CONTACT SYSTEM

The suggestions below describe steps for building an employer contact system using file folders and three-ring notebooks. This same framework can be modeled on most commercial database computer programs.

1. Create and label card file dividers using occupational category labels that are relevant to the labor market in your community (e.g., automotive, building trades, landscape). Organize these file dividers in a cabinet, box, or other container system that allows program staff to easily access and use your employer contact files.

2. Create and produce copies of an employer contact card. Use the sample depicted below or create another version that works for your program. Arrange your employer contact cards in the appropriate files as you make contacts with employers.

3. As you contact employers and fill out the site screening form, compile them in a three-ring notebook for easy access and quick reference. You can update the screening sheets as necessary, making notes about worksite issues or suggestions for helping a new employee find success at this site. (Use of the site screening form is described in the body of Chapter 3 and a sample site screening form is depicted in Appendix 3.5.)

4. Divide your card file and your screening notebook into Active and Inactive sections. The active section includes employers whom you are currently working with, and inactive section will include those employers you have contacted but are not currently pursuing.

5. It is very important that all contact information and placement activities be carefully documented. Employers must have confidence in you and your program, so above all else design and develop an employer contact system that is useful to program staff.

Sample Employer Contact Card

Company Name: _____   Contact Person: _____

Type of Business: _____   Phone #: _____

Address: _____   No. of Employees: _____

Describe Contact with Employer: _____

_____

Results/Next Steps: _____

_____

Signature:_____   Date: _____

APPENDIX 3.2
SAMPLE YTP BROCHURE

"Building Bridges"

Youth Transition Program

. . . involving the community in a new school-to-work program meeting the needs of students and employers.

In cooperation with:

Santa Clara School District
North High School
South High School
NCC Transition Program
Vocational Rehabilitation Division

Students in the YTP program receive on the job training at a paid job, classroom instruction and assistance with planning for life after high school

The YTP Team

Santa Clara School District
Teacher Coordinator
Patty Sand
(555) 555-5555
Transition Specialist
Melissa Smith
(555) 555-5555
Vocational Rehabilitation Division
Frank White
(555) 555-5555
Youth Transition Program
470 Greenhill Rd.
Santa Clara, Oregon 90000
Phone (555) 555-5555
FAX (555) 555-5555

Benefits to Students

- Students participate productively in society, gaining skills that will assist them toward adult independence.

- Students who are hired earn income that will help achieve independent living.

- Students are matched to a job assuring that employers & students benefit from services.

- Students develop the confidence and self-esteem associated with holding a job.

- Students learn new job skills that will improve their employability.

Benefits to the Community

- A valuable school/community partnership is established to help develop a more highly skilled work force.

- Participation in the program increases the probability that young people will become productive citizens who are assets to their community.

Benefits to the Employer

- Time and money are saved on recruiting qualified employees. Students are thoroughly screened and evaluated before they are placed on the job.

- On the job training may be provided to teach and monitor work performance when needed.

- Employers may potentially earn tax credits for employing individuals with disabilities.

- Employers become part of an important school/business partnership that assures students a successful transition from school to adult living.

- Employers get support in training student employees.

- Employer learns new training ideas.

For more information, please call (555) 555-5555

The YTP is providing new options for students with mild disabilities as they transition from high school to the community.

YTP Services

- We contact the employer regarding YTP and discuss jobs available at the work place.

- We analyze the job for specific tasks. This is an important tool which enables the job trainer to expedite the training on the job.

- We match the student's skills, interests, abilities, and other characteristics to an appropriate job.

- We provide initial instruction and training to the student on the job.

- We provide assistance and new skills training to the worker when needed.

- We provide ongoing consulting services in training student workers.

- We provide training in independent living skills.

APPENDIX 3.3
LETTER OF INTRODUCTION FOR PROGRAM

Dear [Employer Name]:

Improving the work readiness and competitiveness of the workforce is important for your business and our community. I am writing to tell you about the Youth Transition Program (YTP), a youth employment training program operated by your local school district. The YTP is an innovative collaboration between the school district, several agencies in our community, and local employers. The YTP offers several services and benefits to employers:

Services Provided by the YTP:

- Students are thoroughly screened and evaluated before they are placed onto a job.
- YTP staff from the school district provide initial training and supervision on the job.
- YTP personnel communicate regularly with employers to ensure student–employee success.

Benefits to Participating Employers:

- You save time and money on recruiting qualified entry-level employees.
- You are assured that employees hired through the YTP are trained and supervised *from the start.*
- You are part of a school/community partnership that prepares students to be competent, competitive members of our community's workforce.

I have enclosed a brochure describing the program in more detail. A staff member from the YTP will be calling in a few days to set up an appointment to discuss your participation in our program. Our students and staff are excited about this program and the prospect of our working together in the future.

Sincerely,

Jane Johnson
YTP Teacher Coordinator
Anyplace School District

APPENDIX 3.4
SITE SCREENING FORM

Name of Company:_____ Date:_____

Address: _____

_____ Phone:_____

Contact Person/Title: _____ Best Contact Time:_____

Description of Business:_____

_____

Types of Jobs Available:_____

_____

Is work site easily accessible by public transportation?   YES ☐   NO ☐

	Poor	Fair	Good
Supervision Provided (Is supervision adequate for student needs?)	☐	☐	☐
Employer's Attitude (Is the employer flexible and open to hiring youth?)	☐	☐	☐
Work Environment (Is the enviroment clean, well organized, and safe?)	☐	☐	☐
Co-worker Support (Are there opportunities for co-workers to provide support?)	☐	☐	☐

Is this employer interested in . . . (check all that apply)
☐ having students tour or "job-shadow"
☐ talking to students at a class
☐ serving as a volunteer mentor
☐ placing students in work experience positions
☐ hiring students as paid employees

Comments: _____

Signature:_____

APPENDIX 3.5
EMPLOYER THANK YOU LETTER

Dear [Employer Name]:

I wanted to write you to express my appreciation for your time and interest in learning about the Youth Transition Program (YTP). I enjoyed our meeting and the opportunity to learn more about your business.

Paragraph for employers not currently interested in working with your program:

In the next few weeks, we will be screening students for participation in the YTP, and working with local employers to provide these students the training and support they will need to become productive and competitive members of our community's workforce. Even though we will not be working together at this point in time, the information I gained from our conversation will be helpful to our staff in carrying out these activities. Thank you again for taking time to talk with me.

Paragraph for employers who are interested in working with your program:

In the next few weeks, we will be screening students for participation in the YTP and working with local employers to provide these students the training and support they will need to become productive and competitive members of our community's workforce. Based on our conversation, we would very much like to talk with you further about:

- ☐ having students visit your business
- ☐ arranging a time for you to talk with our students
- ☐ becoming part of our mentoring program
- ☐ placing students in work experience positions
- ☐ hiring students

I, or another YTP staff member, will contact you in the near future. Again, let me thank you for taking time to talk with me.

Sincerely,

Jane Johnson
YTP Teacher/Coordinator
Anyplace School District

APPENDIX 3.6
RESUME WORKSHEET

Name: _____ Social Security #: _____

Address: _____ Phone #: _____

Work Experience:

Job Title: _____   Job Duties: _____

Employer: _____   _____

City/State: _____   _____

Start/End Dates: _____   _____

Job Title: _____   Job Duties: _____

Employer: _____   _____

City/State: _____   _____

Start/End Dates: _____   _____

Education (Grade/High School/City & State): _____

_____

Skills & Experience: _____

_____

References:

Name: _____ Phone: _____

Address: _____

Name: _____ Phone: _____

Address: _____

APPENDIX 3.7
TYPICAL INTERVIEW QUESTIONS

1. Tell me about yourself.

_____

_____

2. Why do you want to work here?

_____

_____

3. Where do you see yourself in five years?

_____

_____

4. Why should I hire you?

_____

_____

5. What are your strengths?

_____

_____

6. What are your weaknesses?

_____

_____

7. Why did you leave your last job?

_____

_____

(Continues)

8. What did you like most about your last job?

_____

_____

9. How are you qualified for this job?

_____

_____

10. What do you know about our company?

_____

_____

11. How soon could you start?

_____

_____

12. Do you have any questions for me?

_____

_____

APPENDIX 3.8
STUDENT JOB CONTACT SHEET

Date	Company Name and Address	Contact Person Name & Phone #	Call Back	Application Submitted	Interview Scheduled	Follow-Up/ Comments

APPENDIX 3.9
JOB SUMMARY FORM

Company Name: _____ Date: _____

Job Available: _____

Work Days/Hours Required: _____

Wages/Benefits: _____

Job Duties: _____

_____

_____

Specialized Skills Required: (Check all that apply.)

Interpersonal/Communication Skills
- ☐ working with the public
- ☐ answering the telephone
- ☐ working as a member of a team
- ☐ following verbal directions
- ☐ other_____

Functional Academic Skills
- ☐ operating cash register
- ☐ counting change
- ☐ completing paperwork/forms
- ☐ following written directions
- ☐ other_____

Physical Dexterity/Strength
- ☐ repeated bending/lifting
- ☐ standing for extended periods
- ☐ operating heavy equipment
- ☐ using specialized tools
- ☐ working quickly
- ☐ other _____

Other Job-Specific Skills
- ☐ working independently
- ☐ _____
- ☐ _____
- ☐ _____
- ☐ _____
- ☐ _____

Comments: _____

_____

Staff Member Collecting Information: _____

APPENDIX 3.10
STUDENT THANK YOU LETTER

Dear [Employer Name]:

Thank you for taking time to interview me for the position of [insert name of position]. I am very interested in the position and would work hard to meet the demands required of the job. I enjoyed meeting you and look forward to further discussing with you how I could fulfill your employment needs at [insert name of company].

Sincerely,

APPENDIX 3.11
JOB DUTIES CHECKLIST

Student: _____   Job Site: _____

Job Title:_____   Work Hours: _____

Special Tools, Clothing or Equipment Needed: _____

_____

Job Accommodations/Special Training Needed: _____

_____

List specific job duties below:

1.	
2.	
3.	
4.	
5.	
6.	
7.	
8.	
9.	
10.	
11.	
12.	

Comments:_____

_____

_____

APPENDIX 3.12
TRAINING AGREEMENT

Student Name: _____ Phone: _____ Date: _____

Address: _____ Birth Date: _____ SS#: _____

Company Name: _____ Supervisor: _____

Address:_____ Phone: _____

Work Permit Complete: _____ Work Schedule: Days/Hours _____ Starting Rate $_____

The *Student–Worker* agrees to:

1. Keep regular attendance both in school and on the job and not work on any weekday the student does not attend school unless the school absence is authorized by the coordinator. Notify the coordinator and the employer if unable to report as scheduled.
2. Show honesty, punctuality, courtesy, a cooperative attitude, proper health and grooming habits, good dress, and willingness to learn.
3. Consult the coordinator about any difficulties arising at the training station.
4. Conform to the rules and regulations of the work site.
5. Furnish the coordinator with all the necessary information, reports, and weekly time sheets.
6. Maintain passing grades in the job-related class.
7. Authorize release of school and other records.

Student-Worker Signature: _____ Date: _____

The *Parent* agrees to:

1. Encourage the student–worker to effectively carry out job duties and responsibilities.
2. Share the responsibility for the conduct of the student–worker while in the program.
3. Be responsible for the safety and conduct of the student–worker while traveling to and from school, the training station, and home.

Parent Signature: _____ Date: _____

The *School District Program Staff* agree to:

1. Visit and evaluate the student's progress at the work site.
2. Assist in solving problems relating to student's work.
3. Help a student relate in-school learning experiences to work.
4. Provide on-the-job training.
5. Grant credit after satisfactory performance of job duties and completion of requirements in the job-related class as determined by the school and the employer.

Program Representative Signature: _____ Date: _____

The *Employer/Supervisor* agrees to:

1. Employ the student–learner approximately _____ hours each week.
2. Conform to all federal and state regulations regarding employment, safety, child labor laws, minimum wage (if applicable) and other pertinent regulations.
3. Consult the job trainer about problems related to the student's work.
4. Provide time for evaluation and consultation with the job trainer and the student.

Employer/Supervisor Signature: _____ Date: _____

The *Vocational Rehabilitation Counselor* agrees to:

1. Provide consultation and guidance to student job trainer, teacher, parent, and employer, as needed.
2. Assist student/school staff in areas identified to facilitate the attainment of and maintenance of competitive employment.

Rehabilitation Counselor Signature: _____ Date: _____

APPENDIX 3.13
SELF-MONITORING CHECKLISTS

Self-Monitoring Forms—Explanation of Use

Example 1: CNA Job Duties Checklist

This checklist was used in a case where the student was having difficulty staying on task and completing his/her daily requirements at work.

Example 2: Hints for Appropriate Conversation

This student was having difficulty initiating appropriate conversations with senior patients. This sheet contained some prompts to help him/her get started.

Example 3: Bed Making Checklist

This student also had difficulty making the beds properly. The bed making sign was kept with the student and used as a reference when making beds. The staff support person visited the job many times and assisted the student in the procedure before withdrawing support and leaving only the sign for reference.

Example 4: Daily Work Report

This form assisted a student who was having problems with attitude and appropriate behavior on the job. The list included goals that were natural and easy for the student to achieve along with some goals that really needed work. The easily attainable goals allowed the student to have some guaranteed positive feedback as well as remaining aware of areas that needed improvement.

CNA Job Duties Checklist

Name: _____ Date: _____

Job Duty	Yes	No	How Many Times
Arrive on time			
Leave "personal life subjects" outside			
Open staff book			
Find today's date			
Read all new notes			
Write down correct arrival time on time sheet			
Find progress notebooks			
Find yesterday's date			
Read all progress notes on residents			
Take notes on note sheet			
Greet residents cheerfully			
Find something nice to say to residents			
Go to the kitchen			
Check today's menu			
Prepare correct breakfast			
Work quietly and quickly			
Check notes on menu changes			
Serve breakfast to residents			
Find something nice to say to residents			
Ask residents if they want anything else			
Can they have it?			
Clear table			
Work quietly and quickly; "smile"			
Rinse and wash dishes			
Load dishwasher			
Clean table			
Clean counters			

(Continues)

Job Duty	Yes	No	How Many Times
Clean sink			
Start dishwasher			
Check floor, sweep if needed			
Say something pleasant to resident			
Check daily bed schedule			
Strip beds and change them for that day			
Check for wrinkles			
Take dirty sheets to laundry			
Make other residents' beds			
Check for wrinkles			
Ask supervisor for shower schedule			
Check notes for changes in walking			
Say something cheery to resident			
Assist resident in showering			
Use appropriate conversation			
Ask supervisor for additional work			
Work quietly and cheerfully			

Hints for Appropriate Conversation

You look nice today.

That color _____ looks good on you.

Did you enjoy your ___(food)___ ?

Your eyes sure are bright today!

Wow, that (sweater, bathrobe, shirt) looks warm!

Is there something I can get you?

You look so refreshed after your (bath, nap) . Do you feel better?

The weather sure is (hot, chilly, cloudy, foggy, rainy) today.

Smile

Bed Making Checklist

1. Mattress pad   (full length)
2. Bottom sheet   (smooth out wrinkles)
3. Mattress pad   (small)
4. Top sheet   (smooth out wrinkles)
5. Blanket   (check for tag) (smooth out wrinkles)
6. Bed spread   (check for tag) (smooth out wrinkles)

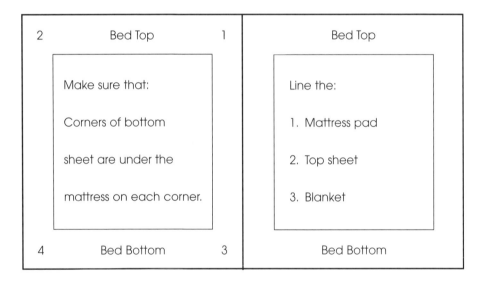

Daily Work Report

Date: _____

	Yes	No
	Yes	No
1. On Time	_____ + 5	— —
2. Neat and Clean	_____ + 5	— —
3. Polite Words	_____ + 5	— —
4. Smile	_____ + 5	— —
5. Good Attitude	_____ + 5	— —
6. Responsible Adult	_____ + 5	— —
7. Worked Hard	_____ + 5	— —
8. Quiet Worker	_____ + 5	— —
9. Kept It in Control	_____ + 10	— —
	(_____) = (_____)

Your total points today are _____

Comments:

Best ever   = 50
Groovy   = 45
Awesome   = 40
Hanging on = 35
30 points and below—
try again tomorrow!

APPENDIX 3.14
CASE NOTE FORM

Student Name:_____   Work Site:_____

Home Phone:_____   Work Phone:_____

Date	Comments

APPENDIX 3.15
MONTHLY PROGRESS REPORT

Student Name: _____ Employment Site:_____

Please rate this individual's current performance in the following areas:

Basic Work Behaviors	Poor	Fair	Good
1. Attends work regularly and calls when unable to go to work.	1	2	3
2. Arrives at work on time and follows break/departure schedule.	1	2	3
3. Follows workplace rules and regulations, including safety rules.	1	2	3
4. Meets expectations for quantity and quality of work.	1	2	3
5. Adjusts to changes in work schedules, routines, or assignments.	1	2	3
6. Maintains good working relationship with co-workers and supervisors.	1	2	3
Specific Job Duties (specify duties)	Poor	Fair	Good
1.	1	2	3
2.	1	2	3
3.	1	2	3
4.	1	2	3
5.	1	2	3
6.	1	2	3
7.	1	2	3
8.	1	2	3

Comments:

Employer/Supervisor Signature: _____ Date: _____

APPENDIX 3.16
SAMPLE SCHOOL–BUSINESS
PARTNERSHIP AGREEMENT

On this _____ day of _____, 19___, a partnership has been entered into by:

_____ and _____
Business   School

for the purposes of sharing resources, improving understanding and communication between a business and a school, and providing opportunities to mutually benefit all participants.

The Partnership Steering Committee and staff hereby acknowledge the existence of this partnership and promise to both support and promote the activities and accomplishments that may result from this association.

The business and school entering into this Agreement pledge to one another the commitment of time, energy, and resources to develop and sustain a viable partnership as outlined in the Partnership Operations Handbook.

The terms and intent of the Agreement will begin with the herein mentioned date and shall remain in effect until terminated by either party upon giving written notice to the other party.

_____   _____
School District Representative   Business Authorization

APPENDIX 3.17
SAMPLE EMPLOYER CONTRACT

Employment Service Partnership Between ABC Products Co. and Anyplace School District

THIS Agreement is made this _____ day of _____, 1996, by and between Anyplace School District, hereinafter referred to as "District," and ABC Products Co., hereinafter referred to as "Company."

Recitals

1. District desires that students from the District participate in on-the-job training as part of the District's vocational education and training program.
2. Company desires to use student interns for packaging and stamping operations at Company's plant.
3. District and Company will enter into a cooperative arrangement whereby District students will become interns for Company performing packaging and stamping operations during regular shifts.
4. The parties desire to specify terms and conditions for the overall agreement.

The Parties agree as follows:

1. District shall:
   a. Recruit and select eligible participants and refer appropriate participants to Company in accordance with available funds, federal regulations, Equal Employment Opportunity laws, needs of participants, and Company job requests.
   b. Provide time sheet forms and instructions to Company, and pay participant's wages according to completed time sheets.
   c. Provide Workers' Compensation Insurance to cover claims by participants for job-related injuries or illnesses.
   d. Provide guidance to the work site and monitor said site to ensure that all provisions of this agreement and any other agreement entered into by Company and District participants are honored.
   e. Terminate, or negotiate modification of this agreement at any time by written notification to Company if its federal, state, or locally

funded grants are suspended, reduced, or terminated before or during the agreement period, or if operation grant terms and/or regulations change significantly.

2. Company shall:
   a. Implement a crew that performs packaging and stamping operations during regular shifts.
   b. Keep an accurate and verifiable record of time spent on the job by each participant and aid participants in submitting time sheets according to the agreed-upon schedule.
   c. Notify District within 24 hours of first learning of an occupational accident or injury affecting any participant.
   d. Call District if problems or concerns arise and/or participant's work is unsatisfactory.
   e. Be permitted to dismiss the participant from the work site for cause, if Company could similarly dismiss its own employees under the same circumstances. Normally, Company would contact District before dismissal. However, in case of an emergency, Company may terminate the participant and then contact District as soon as possible.
   f. Defend, indemnify, and hold the District harmless from and against all claims and demands for loss or damage arising out of, or in any way connected with participant's training and/or performance of his or her job occupation, to the extent permitted by the Oregon Constitution, Article XI, and the provisions of ORS 30.260 through 30.300, except for Workers Compensation coverage.
3. Parties further agree:
   a. That District participants shall be "interns" at Company and will work 4- to 10-hour shifts dependent on their capabilities. The period of work is not to exceed six (6) working months.
   b. At the conclusion of their interning, participants may be hired as full-time or part-time employees for Company.
   c. Termination:
      (1) That by mutual consent this agreement may be terminated at any time.
      (2) In the event of violation of any term of the agreement by either party after five (5) working days written notice.
      (3) For any other reason after giving fourteen (14) working days written notice.

Anyplace School District   **ABC Products Company**

By: _____   By: _____

Date: _____   Date: _____

Anyplace School Temporary Employment Policy

You are a temporary employee of the Anyplace School District, and are expected to follow the rules:

1. All employees are required to have a pre-employment physical examination, including a drug screen.

2. Always be on time for your scheduled shift. If you don't know when you are expected to be at work, contact your supervisor. If you do not show up on time, you can be fired!

3. In case of an emergency where you cannot come to work, notify your supervisor immediately! Failure to report to work is grounds for firing!

4. If you have problems with your schedule, contact your supervisor immediately.

5. If you decide you want to quit your job, you must notify your supervisor two weeks before you want the job to end.

By signing this statement I agree that I have read these rules, understand them, and will follow them.

Signature of Employee _____   Date _____

Supervisor Signature _____   Date _____

Phone Numbers:

Supervisor:

CHAPTER 4

. . . .

Providing Youth with Postprogram Placement and Follow-up Services

. . . .

Congratulations!
Today is your day.
You're off to Great Places!
You're off and away!

You have brains in your head.
You have feet in your shoes.
You can steer yourself any direction you choose.
You're on your own. And you know what you know.
And YOU are the guy who'll decide where to go.

(SEUSS, 1990, PP. 1–2)

Off to great places and new opportunities. The ultimate goal of any school-to-work program is to help students transition into work and further education, and to increase their opportunities to enter first jobs in high-skill, high-wage careers. Earlier in this book we described strategies to help prepare students for that transition through school-based (Chapter 2) and work-based (Chapter 3) learning opportunities. This chapter focuses on connecting activities. Connections between school and work and between school systems and community partners do not happen naturally. Connecting activities are designed to build appropriate links between school and work and from high school to postsecondary education, on-the-job training, employment, or other types of community opportunities.

School-to-work legislation and literature consistently identify the need to create a structured process to help students move from a school environment into the world of work and further learning. Examples of important connecting activities include: (a) providing students support within and across school- and work-based learning opportunities while students are still in school-to-work programs, (b) providing students postprogram planning and assistance to enter and move among postsecondary employment and educational opportunities, and (c) collecting information on student outcomes to monitor and improve program services. Underlying all of these activities is the recognition that without staff resources and support, students often become the only thread that connects schools and postschool opportunities. The importance of this support structure cannot be overstated. Most students leaving school-to-work programs will benefit from some level of support to explore, select, and enter postschool work and continuing education options. These services are essential for youth with special needs given the obstacles that many of these youth must overcome to succeed in the community.

The ideas and strategies described in this chapter focus on two specific types of connecting activities: (a) providing students with postprogram placement support to insure they are well-situated in meaningful competitive employment or career-related postsecondary training, and (b) providing follow-up support services to students after they have left the program to help them manage the complex realities of the adult world. The strategies described in this chapter create a strong bridge between the school and community by providing support and guidance as students transition into employment, independent living, and continuing education environments. Even if a successful link is made to a postschool setting, many young adults experience a floundering period after they leave the predictability of the high school system. Follow-up services provide support and service coordination to help these young adults successfully resolve interpersonal conflicts and explore personal and career goals.

PROVIDING POSTPROGRAM PLACEMENT SERVICES

Postprogram placement is the culminating activity for the school-to-work services provided to youth. All of the other services described in this book are designed to help students reach this critical point—the transition from school to appropriate jobs, continuing education, or additional training programs. But postprogram placement services *should not be isolated events* that happen only when students are ready to leave your school-to-work program. Rather, it should be *a step in the process* of helping students make the transition from school to a postschool environment. This process differs from the way graduation traditionally is viewed. In most high school programs, students work to earn enough credits to graduate. That is the focus— and often the sole focus—of their efforts, and little thought and planning occurs beyond the need to graduate. Unfortunately, when this happens many students experience the same confusion about the purpose of education and the meaning of graduation as Cathy in the cartoon below.

Postprogram placement services should be part of a process that begins when students enter your school-to-work program. It should be a process driven by the individualized plan students create, accomplished through the school- and work-based learning opportunities in which students participate, and reinforced or revised by the follow-up services students receive after they leave the program. The ideas and strategies described in this section are based on these assumptions. Providing postprogram placement services involves two basic steps: (a) helping students review their progress and determine the need for further services *before* they exit, and (b) helping students finalize their placement and determine the need for any further supports *after* they exit.

Review Student Progress and Determine Need for Further Services

Students set goals and developed plans for the future when they entered your program. Over time you've seen these students experience both failure and success as they've struggled to make those goals a reality. Some students will have different career goals as a function of their experiences in the

CATHY   **by Cathy Guisewite**

program. Ideally, all students will have acquired the knowledge, skills, and information they need to move ahead in their chosen career path.

Helping students review their experiences and progress relative to their goals should happen regularly during the time students are in your program. Ideas and strategies for helping students engage in this review process were described in Chapters 2 and 3. Now is the time for a progress review to determine if the student is ready for program exit. This is an opportunity to talk with the student about goals, program experiences, and the need for any further services.

The importance of this review and exit planning process is documented by our experiences with students in the YTP. We have tracked what has happened to students served by YTP sites across Oregon over the past 6 years, and examined the program characteristics that contribute to better outcomes for youth. The vast majority of students in the YTP are "productively engaged" at the time of program exit, meaning they are either working in the community, enrolled in a postsecondary training program, or participating in some combination of the two. Approximately 63% of the students exited into competitive employment, another 14% were enrolled in postsecondary training, and 20% participated in both work and school. These positive

Table 4.1
Program Characteristics Associated with Better Student Outcomes

At the time of program exit, students were more likely to have obtained a completion document, be working full-time, or be engaged in work/schooling activities if they had:

- been in the program 1½ years or more
- 2 or more jobs in the program
- met their individual transition goals, especially in the areas of
  - transportation
  - independent living
  - social–interpersonal

One year after leaving the program, students were more likely to be working full time or engaged in work/schooling activities if they:

- had obtained a completion document before leaving the program
- were engaged in work or school activities at the time of program exit
- received employment and independent living follow-up services at 6 months
- received educational follow-up services at 6 months *for those students who left the program without a completion document*

trends remain steady over the two years that student experiences are monitored through follow-up contacts. Some of the main program characteristics that contribute to these successful outcomes are listed in Table 4.1.

These findings highlight several important features of the exit planning process and the role of reviewing student experiences. Review of student experiences should focus on the progress students have made relative to their goals. We found that students who were able to accomplish their transition goals *while in the program* were more likely to achieve better outcomes at the time of program exit. Similarly, students who had two or more jobs while in the program were more likely to achieve better outcomes at program exit. By design, these jobs should be related to student-identified career goals. The importance of helping students achieve their educational goals is substantiated by the findings one year after leaving the program. Obtaining a completion document *before* leaving the program is closely related to being productively engaged in work and/or school *after* leaving the program. In most cases students exit the program because they have met all of their goals and no longer need active services. When this occurs, and when students are firmly established in a job or enrolled in career-related postsecondary education at the point of program exit, students are more likely to still be engaged in these productive activities a year after leaving the program.

Table 4.1 also documents the importance of follow-up services and their relationship to students' status at the time of program exit. We will discuss the role of follow-up services in more depth later in this chapter. At this point, however, it is worth noting that follow-up services are important for all youth with special needs whether or not they have exited the program successfully. Follow-up services can make a good situation better, and they can help stabilize and improve a tenuous situation. For example, as the findings at the bottom of Table 4.1 demonstrate, students who left the program *without* a completion document *but who received educational follow-up services at 6 months* were just as likely to be engaged in productive activities as students who left the program with a completion document. This is good news. Despite our best efforts, some special needs youth will leave the program unsuccessfully. They may no longer be interested in participating in the program or may be unwilling to follow through with program expectations. There are a variety of reasons why some students leave unsuccessfully. Review of program accomplishments and exit planning are equally if not more important for these students. To the extent possible, encourage these students to participate in this review process with you.

In the end, the decision to exit a student from the program should be made by a team consisting of the student, the student's parent(s) if appropriate, school-to-work staff, and any adult agency staff who have been involved in providing vocational or transition services to the student. It is important to remember that exit from a school-to-work transition program may or may not coincide with high school graduation. Many students need transition services most during the first few months after they leave high school. This is the time of many critical transitions—from part-time to full-time employment and/or from secondary to postsecondary education. Many students will exit the program *after* these important changes have occurred.

Finalize Postprogram Placement and Determine Any Supports Needed

In most instances, postprogram placement means that a student is working in a meaningful job that satisfies his or her career goals. This may be the same job that the student held while in the program, or it may be a new more permanent position that staff assisted the student in obtaining. Some students may not enter the job market directly but instead may enroll in a postsecondary training program. This training might be offered through a university or community college, or it could be short-term training for a specific occupation such as that provided by a truck driving or beauty school. Some students may choose to work at a part-time job to help pay the bills while going to school to enhance their skills. Whether working or continuing their education, it is important for students to be in a stable position at the time of exit. Students who exit the program in this type of positive situation are much more likely to experience success during the early transition years.

As one YTP student commented, "School-to-work is more than just getting a job. It's a way of making long-range plans." This is especially true at the time of program exit. Even though a student may be employed, the school-to-work process isn't necessarily finished. The Postschool Planning Checklist found in Appendix 4.1 is designed to help you review some critical transition issues to insure that students have the support needed for long-term success. The form, designed as a planning tool for students and staff to complete together, includes sections on employment, continuing education and independent living. Some of the issues you may want to discuss with the student include:

Employment

- Will there be any opportunities for career advancement or further training in this position?

- Are there any concerns or unresolved issues which may prevent the student from maintaining this job?

Continuing Education

- Will the student need any assistance completing application or financial aid forms?

- Does the student know how to access any academic support services needed, such as a study skills center?

- What are the projected timelines for completing the program?

- Who will assist the student with job placement services after the program is completed?

Independent Living

- Does the student have a stable living situation?

- Will the student need any special support to live independently?

Note on the planning form any special services that will be provided and the people who will be responsible for providing the support. Copies of the completed postschool planning form should be given to the student and his or her family. The process of discussing these issues one-to-one also will help prepare the student for the more formal exit planning meeting.

Once you have met with a student to confirm the postschool placement and determine any further support needs, you should schedule an exit planning meeting. At a minimum, this meeting should involve the student and the school-to-work staff who have been involved with coordinating services. This is the student's meeting and he or she should be asked to identify any other key people such as family members or agency personnel who should be invited. Students should have the opportunity to lead the exit planning meeting and facilitate the discussion about next steps. Use the following agenda as a general guide for the meeting.

Sample Agenda for Exit Planning Meeting

1. Welcome/introductions;

2. Review student's current status (education, living, employment, etc.);

3. Discuss goals identified and goals achieved;

4. Determine unmet needs;

5. Discuss plans for next 6 months.

The first part of the exit planning meeting should focus on the student's current situation in employment, continuing education, and independent living accommodations. The second part of the meeting should focus on goals. Review the goals that were identified by the student and those that were accomplished. This is an opportunity to look at progress in many areas of transition and to publicly acknowledge the student's achievements. Even if a student is exiting the program under negative circumstances, it is important to note the goals that may have been achieved, such as obtaining a high school diploma, or passing the driver's license exam. Student's current status and goals achieved can be documented on the Exit Form found in Appendix 4.2.

During the last part of the meeting, the team should identify any transition needs that have not been met through the program. For example, a student may have a goal of living in his or her own apartment that has yet to be achieved. If these unmet needs are still a priority, the student must now assume overall responsibility for achieving those goals, with support from family members and any other community resource people. Discuss how these needs will be addressed over the next 6 months. If extensive unmet needs are identified through this process, the team may want to reconsider the decision to exit the student at this time.

It is important that students understand that even though they are exiting the program they will continue to receive some support from staff. Students are now entering into follow-up status, meaning that staff will check in with students on a regular basis to find out how things are progressing. If a student is having difficulties he or she may get additional support from the school to-work staff or be referred to another agency to get any needed services.

PROVIDING FOLLOW-UP SERVICES

School programs have not typically provided follow-up services to students, but successful school-to-work programs **must** include this component. Research clearly shows that even with a structured process for exit planning and postprogram placement, some students will still need occasional support and service coordination to be successful in the community. These follow-up services provide young adults with a minimal, but very powerful, support system to help them negotiate the complicated issues they encounter both on the job and in other areas of their lives. Follow-up can help students recover from a negative situation (such as helping a student transition into a new job after being fired) or improve an already positive situation (such as assisting a student who is successfully employed in accessing further training to upgrade job skills).

During this follow-up period it is important for students to use all the skills they mastered during the program. Being out in the "real world" is the true test of self-advocacy and self-determination. School-to-work staff should now play a minimal role as students and families take ultimate responsibility for the transition process. In addition to focusing on self-determination, follow-up services also allow young adults to maintain an important personal connection with school staff who know and understand them. This mentoring and advocacy role should continue during the follow-up phase of the program. School-to-work staff provide a stable connection for students and serve as a safety net if they should falter. Follow-up services include (a) regularly scheduled contacts between staff and young adults to document students' experiences during the transition years, and (b) the provision of support services, as needed, to help young adults make significant progress toward independence in the community.

Collect Follow-up Information

Before you begin collecting follow-up information, your team should meet to develop a clear plan for this process. One of the first issues to be resolved is how you will use follow-up data. This information is collected primarily to guide services for individual students. However, this same information also can be summarized and used to evaluate outcomes for all of the students served in your program. You can easily summarize and document the numbers of students who have entered successfully into competitive employment or postsecondary training. This information is very powerful when you are lobbying to maintain school-to-work services for youth with special needs. A more complete description of how to collect and summarize evaluation data is provided in Chapter 5.

You also will need to determine time frames for collecting follow-up data. In Oregon, YTP staff gather information at 6-month intervals for 2 years after program exit. However, you may decide to collect the information more often (e.g., every 3 months), or over a longer time frame (e.g., for 3 years after exit). Next you will need to decide the questions you want answered and the format you will use to collect the information. To help you get started, two different sample follow-up forms are provided in Appendix 4.3 and 4.4.

The follow-up form in Appendix 4.3 is a scripted interview designed to be completed over the telephone or face-to-face. The questionnaire format provides staff with a complete list of questions to ask, encompassing the following transition areas: (a) employment, (b) financial status, (c) continuing education/training, (d) living situation, (e) personal relationships, (f) social adjustment, and (g) personal health. This interview gives staff a very clear structure to follow and covers a broad range of topics. The downside of this questionnaire is that it's very time consuming, taking about 30 minutes per student to complete.

The sample follow-up form in Appendix 4.4 is designed to collect basic information on student status in three areas: employment, education, and living status. This form is much easier to complete but doesn't include the breadth of information you gain from the questionnaire. Each follow-up form includes a final section for staff to document student needs and recommended services. Both of these forms have been used by YTP staff in the past. Although sites in Oregon are now using the short form because it takes less time to complete, some staff still prefer the questionnaire format because it gives guidance on how to ask questions instead of just listing the information needed. You may choose to adopt or adapt either one of these formats, or combine elements of both to best meet the needs of your program.

Once you have finalized your decisions about the format of the follow-up form and the time frames for collecting information, your staff will need to begin contacting students to set up an interview time. Ideally, students will remember that the provision of follow-up services was discussed at the exit planning meeting and will be willing and interested in sharing their experiences with staff. This certainly has been the situation with YTP sites in Oregon. When you contact students to set up the interview, remind them of the purpose of the follow-up contact. Explain that during this follow-up contact, students will be asked a series of questions and given a chance to indicate if they need any help to be successful in the community.

When you are conducting the follow-up interview, be sure that students understand the questions you are asking them. You may need to ask a question in more than one way to get complete and accurate information. Record all of the information you collect on the follow-up forms. Remember also that this is an opportunity to check in with the student. Allow time for the students to ask questions and talk about any other issues that are not included on your follow-up form. If you are unable to locate a student to make a follow-up contact, you may still be able to find out how they are doing by talking with the student's parent(s) or friends. Students may also just "drop-in" unexpectedly to talk about how they are doing. Although these unexpected visits are rarely documented using a follow-up form, they are an important aspect of follow-up services.

Provide Follow-up Services as Needed

The follow-up process provides an opportunity to determine a student's status and needs. As one YTP staff member commented, "Teachers use follow-up as a barometer, to get a sense if students are floundering or if they are on the right track." Based on our experiences, most students require a minimal level of follow-up support. Tables 4.2, 4.3, and 4.4 provide information on former YTP students who requested and received assistance at four different points in the follow-up process: 6 months, 1 year, 18 months, and 2 years after program exit.

Looking at Table 4.2, you can see that a quarter (25%) of students received help with employment issues 6 months after leaving the YTP. Fourteen percent received help with educational issues, and 9% received help with financial and independent living issues. The areas in which students requested the most help remained constant over 2 years. Students

Table 4.2
Areas in Which YTP Students Received Follow-up Services Over Time

Areas in Which Services Were Received	Time Since Exiting Program			
	6 months (n = 341)	12 months (n = 234)	18 months (n = 150)	24 months (n = 97)
Employment	25%	22%	19%	17%
Education	14%	9%	11%	4%
Financial/Living	9%	7%	3%	3%
Personal/Family	5%	5%	1%	2%
Medical	4%	5%	1%	1%

always requested the most help with employment issues, followed by continuing education, financial and independent living issues, personal/family issues, and medical health issues. The percentage of students who needed help in these areas diminished gradually over time.

Examples of specific follow-up services in each of these categories are listed in Table 4.3. The services are listed in rank order from those most fre-

Table 4.3
Examples of Follow-up Services Provided to YTP Students

Employment Services

- share job leads and referrals, assistance with job search
- troubleshoot problems on the job
- referral to another agency, such as VRD or Employment Division
- provide job training on a specific skill
- assist with a job change or promotion
- provide social support or referral to job club

Continuing Education Services

- provide guidance and/or counseling about continuing education options
- referral to a specific training program or class
- provide assistance with application or financial aid
- tutoring on a specific subject/support to obtain a completion document

Financial and Independent Living Services

- assistance with budgeting or financial planning
- referral for specific instruction in independent living skills (e.g., driving lessons)
- assistance finding affordable housing

Personal/Family Support Services

- general support or counseling
- assistance with living situation
- referral to an agency for specific service (e.g. family planning)

Medical Support Services

- referral to doctor or dentist
- general support or information

quently provided to those least frequently provided. While not exhaustive, this list illustrates the types of services your staff may need to offer. The support YTP staff provided to help students with these issues included a few telephone conversations or face-to-face meetings to provide information, problem solving support, or referral to an agency for specific training or other related services. For a small percentage of students, follow-up services involved more active intervention to assist with a pending or current crisis situation. If staff know that a student is about to get fired from a job or evicted from an apartment, providing immediate, short-term assistance to resolve the situation can help the student avoid a crisis and stay on course toward achieving long-term goals.

Table 4.4 provides another perspective on students' need for follow-up support. The information in this Table makes it clear that a majority of YTP students needed no help at all during the first 2 years after leaving the program. Almost two-thirds (65%) of students needed no assistance at all 6 months after leaving the YTP. Of the 35% who received help, 20% requested help in only one of the five areas examined during follow-up (e.g., employment, education, independent living). Only 15% of students needed help in two or more areas. Finally, the percentage of students needing help during follow-up diminished gradually over time.

So what should we conclude about the importance of follow-up support as part of school-to-work services for youth with special needs? First, follow-up services are critically important. The information presented earlier in this chapter in Table 4.1 documents that receiving follow-up services is directly related to better outcomes for youth. The information in Table 4.3 indicates that approximately a third of all youth need follow-up support during the

Table 4.4
Number of Follow-up Services Received Over Time

Number of Areas in Which Services Were Received	Time Since Exiting Program			
	6 months (n = 341)	12 months (n = 234)	18 months (n = 150)	24 months (n = 97)
0	65%	70%	75%	82%
1	20%	18%	16%	11%
2	11%	8%	7%	3%
3 to 5	4%	4%	2%	3%

first year after leaving a school-to-work program (i.e., 35% at 6 months and 30% at 1 year). It is worth noting that these percentages most likely *under-estimate* the importance of follow-up and the percentage of students who need this support. The percentages we've been using in these tables are based on a single point in time during which information was collected (e.g., 6 months or 1 year). Any services provided to students outside of these fol-low-up contact points are not captured in this information. Moreover, there is a value to follow-up that goes beyond the percentages reported in these tables. Again, these percentages indicate the number of students who *for-mally* requested and received specific follow-up services such as those described in Table 4.3. We know from direct experience in communities across Oregon that many former students "drop by" for *informal* visits and discussions with staff *because they know staff are interested and committed to them even when they are no longer receiving active school-to-work services.* The importance and value of this aspect of follow-up is immeasurable.

Second, follow-up support must be individualized and responsive to the specific needs of youth. The preceding information clarifies that some young adults will need no assistance at any given time and others will need considerable help. If substantial needs are identified through the follow-up interview, the team should work with the student to develop an individu-alized plan of support. This plan may involve referral to a community agency for further vocational counseling and guidance, on the job training, or other support services, or school-to-work staff may provide some of these services directly. Regardless of which strategies are used, follow-up services should emphasize the concept of student self-determination. Instead of pro-viding all of the answers, staff are more effective if they help students iden-tify possible solutions, and provide the least level of support necessary to help young adults carry out those solutions. Your program has seen these students through a long process—from the time of intake and planning, through work-based and school based learning options, and now into the final stages of exit planning and postprogram placement. Follow-up is a way of ensuring that students are self-reliant and productive as they live and work in the community. Will they succeed? Returning to the words of Dr. Seuss (1990), "Yes indeed!"

> *On and on you will hike*
> *And I know you'll hike far*
> *and face up to your problems*
> *whatever they are.*

So be sure when you step,
step with care and great tact
and remember that Life's
a Great Balancing Act.
Just never forget to be dexterous and deft.
And never mix up your right foot with your left.

And will you succeed?
Yes you will, indeed!
(98 and 3/4 percent guaranteed.)

So. . .
Be your name Buxbaum or Bixby or Bray
or Mordecai Ali Van Allen O'Shea,
you're off to great places!
Today is your day!
Your mountain is waiting.
So. . . Get on your way!

(SEUSS, 1990, PP. 39–40, 42)

APPENDIX 4.1
POSTPROGRAM PLANNING FORM

Student _____ Projected Exit Date_____

Current Address/Phone _____

Career Goals _____

Employment		
Current Status	Training/Supports Needed	Person Responsible

Continuing Education		
Current Status	Training/Supports Needed	Person Responsible

Independent Living		
Current Status	Training/Supports Needed	Person Responsible

Other Comments/Additional Needs: _____

APPENDIX 4.2
EXIT FORM

Name: _____ Date of program exit: ___/___/___

Student Status at Exit

1. Why did this student exit the program?

    a. Permanently employed
    b. Enrolled in postsecondary training
    c. Served by adult agency
    d. Moved/unable to locate
    e. Client declined further services
    f. Lack of follow-through/uncooperative

2. What is the student's current educational status?

Status and Type of Classes	Location of Program
1. Not Enrolled 2. Currently dropped out of school 3. Taking classes for a high school diploma 4. Taking classes for GED 5. Classes for adult basic ed./remedial educ. 6. Life skills classes 7. Academic/vocational classes for postsecondary degree or certificate 8. Vocational skill training/Job Corp 9. Other _____	1. High School 2. Community College 3. 4-yr College or University 4. Voc. training facility/Job Corp 5. Other _____

3. What type of completion document has the student received?

    a. None   e. Vocational certificate
    b. High school diploma   f. A.A. degree
    c. GED   g. Other _____
    d. Graduation certificate

4. What was the student's **living** status at the time he/she exited the program?

    a. Alone   d. With roommates
    b. With parents/family   e. Vocational/residential training facility
    c. With spouse/partner   f. Other _____

(Continues)

5. What was this student's **employment** status at the time he/she exited the program?
   a. Not employed
   b. Unpaid work experience placement
   c. Working part-time (< 35 hours/week)
   d. Working full-time (35+ hours/week)

Record all job information in the table on the next page.

7. What is the student's current **income source**? (Circle all that apply)
   a. Wages
   b. Social Security (SSI, SSDI)
   c. Public assistance (food stamps, welfare)
   d. Family/relatives
   e. Other _____

8. Is the student having any **personal or family problems?** No ☐ Yes ☐ (Circle all that apply)
   a. Unstable family situation
   b. Lacks friends/social networks
   c. Victimization/harassment/abuse
   d. Problems in relationship with spouse/partner
   e. Problems with anger management
   f. Other _____

9. Is the student having any **health or medical problems?** No ☐ Yes ☐ (Circle all that apply)
   a. Depression
   b. Problems with substance abuse
   c. Unplanned pregnancy
   d. Needs psychiatric/mental health services
   e. Needs info/access to health insurance
   f. Needs family planning/birth control
   g. Needs medical care
   h. Needs dental care
   i. Other _____

(Continues)

Employer	Job title/ duties	Start date	End date	Hourly wage (enter wage or circle one)	Hrs. per week	Benefits (circle all that apply)	Reason for termination
				1. Wage:$_____ 2. Unpaid work exp. 3. Salary + room or board		1. None 2. Vacation 3. Sick time 4. Medical 5. Dental 6. Retirement	1. Fired 2. Laid off 3. Quit 4. School/ temp job ended
				1. Wage:$_____ 2. Unpaid work exp. 3. Salary + room or board		1. None 2. Vacation 3. Sick time 4. Medical 5. Dental 6. Retirement	1. Fired 2. Laid off 3. Quit 4. School/ temp job ended

Student Goals

For each transition area below, circle all of the goals that were met or completed.

Employment Goals:

1. No employment goals
2. Complete vocational evaluation
3. Attend job club/support group
4. Participate in unpaid work experience
5. Obtain part-time employment
6. Obtain full-time employment
7. Enlist in military
8. Other _____

Continuing Education Goals:

1. No continuing education goals
2. Complete high school diploma
3. Enroll in life-skills classes
4. Complete GED/adult HS diploma
5. Enroll in academic/voc. classes for postsecondary degree or certificate
6. Enroll in vocational program/classes
7. Other _____

Financial Security Goals:

1. No financial goals
2. Apply for Social Security (SSI)
3. Apply for public assistance (food stamps, welfare)
4. Open a checking/savings account
5. Learn money mgmt.
6. Other _____

Independent Living Goals:

1. No independent living goals
2. Live with parents/family
3. Live independently (alone/with roommates or spouse/partner)
4. Learn IL skills (e.g., cooking, shopping)
5. Other _____

Transportation Goals:

1. No transportation goals
2. Enroll in driver's education
3. Obtain driver's permit
4. Obtain driver's license
5. Use public transportation
6. Purchase a bicycle/moped
7. Purchase a car
8. Other _____

Family/Social Relationship Goals:

1. No family/social goals
2. Develop/maintain friendships
3. Develop/maintain family relationships
4. Improve social skills
5. Obtain counseling for personal relationship
6. Other _____

(Continues)

Physical/Mental Health Goals:

1. No physical/mental health goals
2. Improve fitness/health/hygiene
3. Enroll in weight loss program
4. Enroll in drug/alcohol rehabilitation
5. Receive counseling
6. Other _____

Leisure/Recreation Goals:

1. No leisure/recreation goals
2. Develop a hobby
3. Participate in recreation activities
4. Plan leisure activities with friends
5. Other _____

Social/Civic Responsibility Goals:

1. No social/civic goals
2. Register to vote
3. Volunteer for civic/community activities
4. Maintain terms of parole
5. Other _____

APPENDIX 4.3
FOLLOW-UP QUESTIONNAIRE

Site_____ Date_____

Client_____ SSN_____

Instructions: Circle the number associated with the client's response or fill in the blank with the client's answer.

The first questions in this interview are related to any jobs that you have had in the last 6 months.

1. During the past 6 months, have you had any jobs?

    (1) Yes   (2) No (Skip to Question 22)

2. How many jobs have you had during the past 6 months?

    _____ (Enter number of jobs)

3. What is the name of the most recent job you had?

    Position_____

I'd like to know a little more about this job.

4. What did you do on the job? _____

    _____

5. How many hours did you work each week?_____

6. How much did you make per hour? _____

7. When did you start this job?

    (1) More than 6 months ago
    (2) Within the last 6 months (Enter month and year below)

    Month _____(Beg. _____ End _____) Year _____

8. Are you still working?

    (1) Yes   (2) No

    (If client had more than one job, skip to Question 11; if client had only one job, skip to Question 18.)

(Continues)

9. When did you leave this job? (Enter month and year below)

   Month _____(Beg. _____ End _____)   Year _____

10. Why did you leave your job?

    (1) Quit (Circle all reasons that apply)
       a. Didn't like some part of the job
       b. Didn't like co-workers
       c. Didn't like boss
       d. Trouble doing the job
       e. Transportation problems getting to the job
       f. Offered another job
       g. Other: _____

    (2) Fired or laid off (Circle all reasons that apply)
       a. Didn't get along with co-workers
       b. Didn't get along with supervisor
       c. Couldn't perform job duties at appropriate skill level
       d. Excessive absences and/or tardies
       e. Transportation problems getting to the job
       f. Lack of work and/or economic slow down
       g. Other: _____

    (Skip to question 18 if client had only one job)

Now, I'd like to know more about the other job you had.

11. What was the name of the job you had?

    Position _____

12. What did you do on the job? _____

    _____

13. How many hours did you work each week? _____

14. How much did you make per hour? _____

15. When did you start this job?

    (1) More than 6 months ago
    (2) Within the last 6 months (Enter month and year below)

       Month _____(Beg. _____ End _____)   Year _____

16. When did you leave this job? (Enter month and year below)

    Month _____(Beg. _____ End _____)   Year _____

(Continues)

17. Why did you leave your job?
    (1) Quit (Circle all reasons that apply)
        a. Didn't like some part of the job
        b. Didn't like co-workers
        c. Didn't like boss
        d. Trouble doing the job
        e. Transportation problems getting to the job
        f. Offered another job
        g. Other: _____

    (2) Fired or laid off (Circle all reasons that apply)
        a. Didn't get along with co-workers
        b. Didn't get along with supervisor
        c. Couldn't perform job duties at appropriate skill level
        d. Excessive absences and/or tardies
        e. Transportation problems getting to the job
        f. Lack of work and/or economic slow down
        g. Other: _____

18. Have you been unemployed at all during the past 6 months?
    (1) Yes   (2) No (Skip to Question 20)

19. How many weeks during the past 6 months have you been unemployed?
    _____ (Enter number of weeks)

20. Have you had any problems getting back and forth to work?
    (1) Yes   (2) No

21. Over the past 6 months, have you been happy with the way things have gone with your job(s)? Would you say . . .
    (1) Usually   (2) Sometimes   (3) Hardly ever   (4) Don't know

22. Do you want any help from us in finding or keeping a job during the next 6 months?
    (1) Yes
    (2) No (Skip to Question 24)
    (3) Don't know (Skip to Question 24)

23. What kind of help would you like?

    _____

(Continues)

The next questions are about how you have earned and spent money in the last 6 months.

24. People get money to live on and pay bills from a lot of different places. During the last 6 months, did you get money from . . . (Circle all that apply)

    (1) Work
    (2) Worker's compensation after injury
    (3) Unemployment benefits after being laid off
    (4) Food stamps (that you have applied for)
    (5) Section VIII housing subsidy
    (6) Social security (SSI or SSDI)
    (7) Public welfare (Adult/Family Services)
    (8) Student loan/bank loan
    (9) Family/relative
    (10) Income from spouse's job
    (11) Vocational Rehabilitation
    (12) Other: _____

25. During the past 6 months have you had enough money to pay the bills? Would you say . . .

    (1) Usually   (2) Sometimes   (3) Hardly ever   (4) Don't know

26. Are you happy with how much money you have for other things besides paying bills? Would you say . . .

    (1) Usually   (2) Sometimes   (3) Hardly ever   (4) Don't know

27. Do you want any help from us with your finances during the next 6 months?

    (1) Yes
    (2) No (Skip to Question 29)
    (3) Don't know (Skip to Question 29)

28. What kind of help would you like?

    _____

The next set of questions deals with any training or additional education which you may have had in the last 6 months.

29. During the past 6 months did you attend a school or training program?

    (1) Yes   (2) No (Skip to Question 38)

(Continues)

30. Were you enrolled as a full-time or part-time student?

    (1) Full-time _____   (2) Part-time _____

31. What type of classes or training did you attend? (If more than one, circle the most recent)

    (1) High school diploma
    (2) G.E.D.
    (3) Adult Basic Education/remedial studies
    (4) Vocational training program
    (5) Regular academic postsecondary classes

32. Where did you get this training? (If more than one, circle the most recent)

    (1) High school
    (2) Community college
    (3) Vocational-technical school
    (4) Job Corps
    (5) Military
    (6) 4-year college
    (7) Other: _____

33. Did you complete the classes you were taking?

    (1) Yes (Skip to Question 35)   (2) No

34. What was the main reason you didn't complete the class(es)?

    (1) Still attending
    (2) Poor grades
    (3) Funding
    (4) Bored/didn't want to be there
    (5) Expelled/discipline
    (6) Employment
    (7) Relocation
    (8) Personal problems
    (9) Coursework too difficult
    (10) Other: _____

(Continues)

35. Have you received any type of diploma, degree, or certificate in the last 6 months?

   (1) Yes (Indicate type of diploma below)   (2) No
       a. High school diploma
       b. Certificate of high school completion
       c. G.E.D.
       d. Vocational training/Apprentice certificate
       e. 2-year AA degree
       f. 4-year degree
       g. Other: _____

36. Have you had any problems getting back and forth to school?

   (1) Yes   (2) No

37. Over the past 6 months have you been happy with your continuing education? Would you say . . .

   (1) Usually   (2) Sometimes   (3) Hardly ever   (4) Don't know

38. Do you want any help from us with your continuing education during the next 6 months?

   (1) Yes
   (2) No (Skip to Question 40)
   (3) Don't know (Skip to Question 40)

39. What kind of help would you like?

   _____

My next few questions are about where you have been living during the last 6 months.

40. Where are you living right now?

   (1)   At home with parents
   (2)   With other relatives/family friend
   (3)   Group home
   (4)   Foster home
   (5)   Semi-independent living situation (satellite apartment)
   (6)   Own home or apartment (including with friend/spouse)
   (7)   Homeless/community shelter
   (8)   Prison/incarcerated
   (9)   Military

(Continues)

(10) Residential training center

(11) Other: _____

41. Have you lived anywhere else in the last 6 months?

    (1) Yes   (2) No (Skip to Question 43)

42. Where else did you live? (Circle all that apply)

    (1) At home of parents
    (2) With other relatives/family friend
    (3) Group home
    (4) Foster home
    (5) Semi-independent living situation (satellite apartment)
    (6) Own home or apartment (including with friend/spouse)
    (7) Homeless/community shelter
    (8) Prison/incarcerated
    (9) Military
    (10) Residential training center
    (11) Other: _____

43. Have you had any problems getting back and forth to the places you need to go in the community?

    (1) Yes   (2) No

44. Have you been happy with your living arrangement over the past 6 months?

    (1) Usually   (2) Sometimes   (3) Hardly ever   (4) Don't know

45. Do you want any help from us with your living situation during the next 6 months?

    (1) Yes
    (2) No (Skip to Question 47)
    (3) Don't know (Skip to Question 47)

46. What kind of help would you like?

    _____

(Continues)

My next questions are about personal relationships that you have with your family and friends.

47. Do you feel you have someone you can talk to if you have a personal or family problem?

    (1) Yes   (2) No (Skip to Question 49)

48. Who is the person you are most likely to talk with?

    (1) Parent
    (2) Other relative
    (3) Spouse
    (4) Friend
    (5) Teacher
    (6) Transition specialist/school-to-work staff
    (7) VR counselor
    (8) Other agency personnel (Specify _____)
    (9) Psychologist/psychiatrist
    (10) Other: _____

49. Do you feel you have friends outside your family?

    (1) Yes   (2) No (Skip to Question 51)

50. Do you think you spend enough time with your friends?

    (1) Yes   (2) No

51. How often have you felt lonely in the last 6 months? Would you say . . .

    (1) Usually   (2) Sometimes   (3) Hardly ever   (4) Don't know

52. Do you want any help from us with your personal or family life during the next 6 months?

    (1) Yes
    (2) No (Skip to Question 54)
    (3) Don't know (Skip to Question 54)

53. What kind of help would you like?

    _____

(*Continues*)

Sometimes young adults may have problems adjusting to their new life in the community. The next questions are about problems you may or may not have. If you don't feel comfortable answering any of these questions, just let me know.

54. Have you been arrested in the past 6 months?

    (1) Yes (Please specify) _____

    (2) No (Skip to Question 56)

55. Did you spend time in jail or detention?

    (1) Yes   (2) No

56. Have you been connected with any type of alcohol or drug rehabilitation program in the last 6 months?

    (1) Yes (Please specify) _____

    (2) No

57. Do you want any help from us to deal with these problems during the next 6 months?

    (1) Yes

    (2) No (Skip to Question 59)

    (3) Don't know (Skip to Question 59)

58. What kind of help would you like?

_____

The last questions are about your personal health.

59. Have you had any major health problems or injuries in the past 6 months?

    (1) Yes (Please specify) _____

    (2) No

60. Do you want any help from us with health or medical needs during the next 6 months?

    (1) Yes

    (2) No (Skip to Question 62)

    (3) Don't know (Skip to Question 62)

61. What kind of help would you like?

_____

(Continues)

62. Can you give me the names and phone numbers of two people who might help us find you if you should move in the next 6 months?

Name _____ Phone_____

Name _____ Phone_____

Those are all the questions I have for you at this time. Do you have anything that you would like to ask me?

Comments _____

_____

_____

Closing Statement

(Option A: If client says they want help in certain areas)

Thanks for taking time to answer these questions. The answers you gave help us have a better idea of how things are going for you now that you have left high school. We would like to have a meeting with you soon so we can talk about how we might help you with some of the problems you have told us about. We will be contacting you soon to set up a time to meet with you. Thanks again.

(Option B: If client does not identify any areas of need)

Thanks for taking time to answer these questions. The answers you gave help us have a better idea of how things are going for you now that you have left high school. It sounds like everything is going really well in your life right now. We will be getting in touch with you again in 6 months to see how you are doing. Be sure to call us if anything comes up that you do need help with. Thanks again.

Follow-up Services To be completed by staff following interview

For each of the areas below, indicate the level of services that will be provided. Check all that apply.

Employment

	No intervention beyond follow-up contact.
	Short-term assistance. Type of assistance:
	Referral to another agency. Agency:
	Long-term assistance. Type of assistance:

Continuing Education

	No intervention beyond follow-up contact.
	Short-term assistance. Type of assistance:
	Referral to another agency. Agency:
	Long-term assistance. Type of assistance:

Financial/Living

	No intervention beyond follow-up contact.
	Short-term assistance. Type of assistance:
	Referral to another agency. Agency:
	Long-term assistance. Type of assistance:

Personal or Family

	No intervention beyond follow-up contact.
	Short-term assistance. Type of assistance:
	Referral to another agency. Agency:
	Long-term assistance. Type of assistance:

Health or Medical

	No intervention beyond follow-up contact.
	Short-term assistance. Type of assistance:
	Referral to another agency. Agency:
	Long-term assistance. Type of assistance:

APPENDIX 4.4
FOLLOW-UP FORM

Name: _____ Date of report _____

Follow-up report: (circle one) #1   #2   #3   #4

Student Status at Exit

1. What is the student's current educational status?

Status and Type of Classes	Location of Program
1. **Not Enrolled** 2. Currently dropped out of school 3. Taking classes for a high school diploma 4. Taking classes for GED 5. Classes for adult basic ed./remedial educ. 6. Life skills classes 7. Academic/vocational classes for postsecondary degree or certificate 8. Vocational skill training/Job Corp 9. Other _____	1. High School 2. Community College 3. 4-yr College or University 4. Voc. training facility/Job Corp 5. Other _____

2. Indicate the type of completion document the student has received since exiting the program
   a. None
   b. High school diploma
   c. GED
   d. High school certificate of attendance/comp.
   e. Vocational skill certificate
   f. A.A. degree
   g. Other _____

3. What is the student's current employment status?
   a. Not employed
   b. Unpaid work experience placement
   c. Working part-time (< 35 hours/week)
   d. Working full-time (35+ hours/week)

(Continues)

Record all job information in the table on the next page.

Financial Living Status

1. Please provide the name and phone of a person who should always know the student's current address:

   Name: _____ Phone # (___) ____-_____

2. Enter the student's current address and phone:

   Street: _____ Phone # (___) ____-_____

   City: _____ State: _____ Zip _____

3. What is the student's current living status?
   a. Alone
   b. With parents/family
   c. With spouse/partner
   d. With roommates
   e. Vocational/residential training facility
   f. Other _____

4. What is the student's current income source? (circle all that apply)
   a. Wages
   b. Social Security (SSI, SSDI)
   c. Public assistance (food stamps, welfare)
   d. Family/relatives
   e. Other _____

5. Is the client having personal or family problems? No ☐ Yes ☐ (circle all that apply)
   a. Unstable family situation
   b. Lacks friends/social networks
   c. Victimization/harassment/abuse
   d. Problems in relationship with spouse/partner
   e. Problems with anger management
   f. Other _____

6. Is the client having any health or medical problems? No ☐ Yes ☐ (circle all that apply)
   a. Depression
   b. Problems with substance abuse
   c. Unplanned pregnancy
   d. Needs psychiatric/mental health services
   e. Needs info/access to health insurance
   f. Needs family planning/birth control
   g. Needs medical care
   h. Needs dental care
   i. Other _____

(Continues)

Employer	Job title/ duties	Start date	End date	Hourly wage (enter wage or circle one)	Hrs. per week	Benefits (circle all that apply)	Reason for termination
				1. Wage:$_____ 2. Unpaid work exp. 3. Salary + room or board		1. None 2. Vacation 3. Sick time 4. Medical 5. Dental 6. Retirement	1. Fired 2. Laid off 3. Quit 4. School/ temp job ended
				1. Wage:$_____ 2. Unpaid work exp. 3. Salary + room or board		1. None 2. Vacation 3. Sick time 4. Medical 5. Dental 6. Retirement	1. Fired 2. Laid off 3. Quit 4. School/ temp job ended

Follow-up Needs/Recommended Services

For each of the areas below, indicate the level of services that will be provided. Check all that apply.

Employment

	No intervention beyond follow-up contact.
	Short-term assistance. Type of assistance:
	Referral to another agency. Agency:
	Long-term assistance. Type of assistance:

Continuing Education

	No intervention beyond follow-up contact.
	Short-term assistance. Type of assistance:
	Referral to another agency. Agency:
	Long-term assistance. Type of assistance:

Financial/Living

	No intervention beyond follow-up contact.
	Short-term assistance. Type of assistance:
	Referral to another agency. Agency:
	Long-term assistance. Type of assistance:

Personal or Family

	No intervention beyond follow-up contact.
	Short-term assistance. Type of assistance:
	Referral to another agency. Agency:
	Long-term assistance. Type of assistance:

Health or Medical

	No intervention beyond follow-up contact.
	Short-term assistance. Type of assistance:
	Referral to another agency. Agency:
	Long-term assistance. Type of assistance:

CHAPTER 5

• •

Managing School-to-Work Programs

• •

When asked what they want from programs, youth say they want secure and stable relationships with caring peers and adults, safe and attractive places to relax and be with their friends, and opportunities to develop life skills, contribute to their communities, and feel competent.

(CARNEGIE COUNCIL ON ADOLESCENT DEVELOPMENT, 1995, P. 108)

Opportunities and relationships. What do these concepts have to do with managing collaborative school-to-work programs? A lot. Program management strategies are tools for insuring that program services are organized and delivered in an effective and efficient manner, and that students are provided meaningful opportunities for success. Effective relationships among staff, students, and other partners lie at the core of program services and meaningful opportunities for students.

One of the purposes of the school-to-work program is to promote partnerships among secondary schools and postsecondary educational institutions, private and public employers, community organizations, parents, and students. The intention of school-to-work is not to create an isolated program, but instead to *build a system* that brings together all of these various resources to meet the needs of students in transition. On paper, collaborative service delivery is a wonderful concept. But just imagine representatives from each of these various agencies actually sitting around the same table and talking to each other about "building a system." Each government agency would bring to the meeting its own set of complicated federal regulations, the educational institutions would have existing policies and programs to consider, the business community would have to think in terms of production and profit, and we haven't even started to talk about the needs of parents and students!

So how can local practitioners pull together these vastly different con-stituents to create truly collaborative programs? It must start with a few key people who have the dedication and perseverance to make it happen. The most successful school-to-work programs have been able to garner the resources to hire staff who are *solely responsible* for school-to-work activities. The primary role of staff is to facilitate opportunities for students and build links with teachers, counselors, agency staff, and employers. The relationships staff build with these partners becomes the glue that holds the system together. To be effective, the school-to-work staff must constantly develop, monitor, and revise the local system. They have to be willing to collaborate with vari-ous agencies, be sensitive to the needs of the business community, and be able to maintain positive relationships with other staff and administrators.

The vignette in Chapter 1 titled "A Day in the Life of a Special Needs School-to-Work Teacher" illustrates the importance of building collabora-tive services with community partners and highlights some of the issues you will face as you develop and manage school-to-work programs in the real world. Go back to Chapter 1 and reread this story if the details are no longer fresh in your memory.

In Chapters 2 through 4 we have described ideas and strategies to help you develop school-based, work-based, and connecting activities. This chap-ter describes strategies for managing and evaluating these activities. For clar-ity, the information in these chapters is presented sequentially. But life is not always so orderly.

On any given day you might be involved with meeting some potential new students, talking with an employer about a structured work experience placement, or teaching a vocational class, while all the time you're thinking about a new school-based enterprise you plan to develop. You'll find yourself working with students at various levels. Some students may be thinking about transition for the first time while others may have been surviving on their own for several years and are ready to come back for some guidance from pro-gram staff.

On a day-to-day basis you may feel as though you're running to make your next appointment. Over time though, as you work with students and staff, your efforts across all of these activities will create the foundation of a com-prehensive program. The remainder of this chapter includes ideas and strate-gies for building a strong foundation for your school-to-work program and collecting evaluation information on the effect of your program on students, the school, and community.

BUILDING THE FOUNDATION

This section describes procedures to help you: (a) develop a collaborative school-to-work team, (b) recruit a pool of students to participate, (c) provide and monitor school-to-work services, and (d) build partnerships with school and community resources. All four of these activities will remain as ongoing management activities once your program is fully operational. As your program grows, or as staff members move on, you will once again need to identify and train staff.

Recruiting students is also a continuous activity. At any one time some of your students will be completing the intake process, others will be actively engaged in employment or training activities, and still others will be in a follow-up status. Part of the challenge of program management is to maintain effective services as you cycle through an ever-changing array of students (and staff).

Develop a Collaborative School-to-Work Team

Develop a plan for staffing the program

The key to building an effective program is identifying the right staff and assigning them the right responsibilities. School-to-work programs can have a variety of staffing patterns. In the YTP model, key school staff include a teacher–coordinator and a transition specialist. The teacher–coordinator is typically a special education teacher or a work experience coordinator who has been reassigned to provide school-to-work services. A YTP teacher coordinator's typical job duties include supervising program staff, providing classroom instruction, managing the program budget, and evaluating the impact of the program. A sample job description for a teacher–coordinator is included in Appendix 5.1.

The other key staff member in the YTP program is the transition specialist. Transition specialists typically are classified staff in the school district whose primary responsibility is to coordinate services for students in transition. They provide job training and support, individualized instruction, and follow-up services, and also serve as the liaison between the student, employer, and other agency staff. A sample job description for a transition specialist position is included in Appendix 5.2. Use these examples to define the roles of your key staff, and develop job descriptions that meet the needs of your program. Once job descriptions have been developed, you will need to review them with key school administrators and obtain the assistance you need to formally recruit applicants to fill these positions. Some programs have been able to reassign existing classroom staff to new duties as school-to-work specialists. Others have found that hiring staff from the community—especially people with direct experience in the business world—brings a fresh perspective to the school program. Whatever approach you use, try to find people who are flexible, energetic, and have the desire to work intensively with young adults.

The formal job descriptions you use as a hiring tool are only a starting point. Your team should identify the critical activities that must be accomplished (such as recruiting students, job placement and training, public relations activities, etc.) and then decide who will take responsibility for each activity. You may want to hold a team brainstorming session at which you list all of the important activities on a chalkboard and negotiate specific responsibilities for each team member. Consider the strengths and interests of each team member when delegating responsibilities. Each staff member should be in a role that complements his or her professional interests and abilities. For example, although the teacher may have overall responsibility for marketing the program within the school, nothing prevents another staff member who enjoys desktop publishing from developing a brochure describing the program. Be flexible in these assignments and remain open to changes in responsibilities over time as staff members' interests and abilities change.

As you develop your staffing plan, remember that you may want to include other staff from adult service agencies as part of your service delivery team. Because the focus of your program is to transition students into the community, it make sense for you to develop strong relationships with staff from community programs, including: (a) vocational rehabilitation counselors and managers, (b) representatives from local job training programs, (c) juvenile corrections staff, (d) community college staff responsible for adult education, or vocational programs, and (e) other key personnel involved in local school-to-work programs. You can invite these additional team members to attend your program meetings once you have established a base of students, or you might want to involve some of them in the initial phases of program development. In the YTP, staff have made a commitment to build a collaborative service delivery model beginning with the student selection process. Since many students in the YTP are also clients of vocational rehabilitation, VR counselors assist in recruiting and screening students for the program. Vocational rehabilitation staff in Oregon also provide vocational assessment, career guidance, and assistance with coordinating services. Combining the strengths of the school staff with the expertise and resources of the community agency creates a collaborative team that can work in the best interests of students.

Develop a plan for meeting as a team and documenting activities

Because they spend so much time working with employers and other community agencies, school-to-work staff can sometimes feel isolated. Regular meetings help reestablish the communication lines and provide support to staff who are "out in the trenches." Key staff from schools and adult agencies should schedule meetings at least once a month to discuss client progress, share information, and resolve any program management issues. Some teams meet as often as once a week, especially during the early phases of developing the program. The most successful teams set regular meeting times (e.g. the first and third Tuesday of every month) and come to meetings prepared with specific issues or concerns to discuss.

The action plan form included in Appendix 5.3 is designed to document the outcomes of these regular team meetings. This form can be used as an informal agenda to record the issues each team member brings to the meeting. It is also designed as a work plan to document the decisions reached and indicate who is responsible for following up on specific tasks.

The last step in building a collaborative team is to develop a system for documenting staff activities. Some programs use time cards, requiring each staff member to record the number of hours worked. Others use a log sheet, where staff note the date and the activities they completed. The activity log in Appendix 5.4 is a combination of those two approaches. Each week YTP staff use the activity log to record the total number of hours engaged in program activities. They also break down their responsibilities into several categories, noting the number of hours spent in each type of activity.

The information you collect through the activity log can be used for several purposes. First, it can function as a time sheet documenting hours worked for payroll purposes. It also can become a useful management tool. Reviewing completed activity logs will help to paint a picture of how your staff members are using their time. As an example, staff in one YTP site were feeling frustrated because so many of their students were not yet employed in the community. After reviewing the activity logs they found that transition specialists were only spending about 2 hours per week working with students on job search activities. Once these activities became a priority for staff, students were much more successful in securing employment.

Recruit a Pool of Students To Participate

Advertise the program with school staff, students, and parents

Advertise your program with school personnel as part of your student recruitment process. Provide information to school administrators, vocational education teachers, special education teachers, alternative education teachers, school counselors, and any other personnel who you think will have some connection with school-to-work programs. Schedule a time to present information at a staff meeting, or if you are more comfortable with small groups you can have informal discussions with one or two staff members at a time. These orientation meetings are a chance to give a brief overview of the students you are targeting for participation, the services you plan to provide, and the outcomes you hope to achieve. It is also important to explain the roles and responsibilities of your staff and the process you will use to identify potential students. Any written information you have developed describing your program should be distributed during these meetings. These initial contacts will help build a strong base of support within the school for your program.

Talking to school staff is only one way to begin to identify potential students. Another approach is to go directly to students. You may want to present information about your program during career or vocational classes, or possibly at club meetings where students with specific interests may gather. Some YTP site staff also have recommended looking for referrals "behind the high school where kids are just hanging out." Sometime these students (or dropouts) are just waiting for the right opportunity to do something with their lives. They may be very attracted to a program that can help them find a job and finish school at the same time. Eventually, as your program gains credibility and visibility, students will begin to refer themselves or their friends.

Meet with students to explain the program and complete any initial paperwork

Once you have complied a list of potential referrals for the program, set times to meet with students, either individually or in small groups. Explain the services available through the program, the responsibilities students will have to fulfill to benefit from the program, and any steps that will be necessary in order to participate (e.g., completing an application). Students should be asked to make a clear commitment to participate. This is a key step in the process because you are assessing student's motivation to participate.

Ask interested students to complete an application. This is an opportunity to collect some basic information about the student's school and employment history. Many programs also use a nomination form to collect additional background information from an adult who knows the student well, such as a teacher, counselor, or case manager. A sample program application is included in Appendix 5.5 and a sample nomination form is included in Appendix 5.6. Finally, for students who may be receiving services from other community agencies, you may need to have students complete a release of information form. By signing this form, students give permission for these organizations to share any information that will be helpful for planning and coordinating services. A sample information release form is included in Appendix 5.7.

Provide and Monitor Services to Students

Provide individualized school-to-work services to students

Now you are ready to begin working with students. Chapters 2 to 4 described ideas and strategies for providing school-to-work services for special needs youth. Your first step should be to facilitate a planning meeting, bringing together the key people in the student's life to talk about the future. This is your opportunity to talk about the student's interests and abilities as well as career and personal goals. This planning process should be flexible enough to meet individual student needs, yet structured enough to provide some clear direction on the next steps for students and staff. Chapter 2 provides ideas and strategies for collecting assessment information and helping students develop long-term and short-term goals.

Monitor student progress on a continuing basis

Student experiences, accomplishments, and progress toward meeting their overall program goals should be monitored on a continuing basis. The best way to monitor student progress is to schedule regular meetings with students.

Some programs require students to check in with staff (either in person or by phone) as often as twice a week. Regular check in times provide an opportunity to consult with students and assist them with solving any pressing needs. Use your judgment and knowledge of students to develop a schedule for monitoring progress. Document any issues that arise during these informal contacts. A sample case note form is included in Appendix 5.8. Every 3 to 6 months, you should also meet with students to more formally review strengths and weaknesses and determine the need for additional learning opportunities. At this time you may want to collect additional assessment data from employers or other school-to-work staff. Collecting evaluation information from employers is discussed in Chapter 3.

Once you have collected this information, you will need a system to organize it. Many programs create case files for each student. Manila folders or three-ring binders will organize all of the critical information about an individual student. Consider including the following information in your student case files:

Intake Information

- Student demographics (name/address/phone/DOB, etc.)
- Completed application
- Copy of nomination form or screening packet
- Pertinent testing/assessment information
- Signed release of information form

Student Goal Setting/Planning

- Documentation of students skills, interests, preferences
- Career goals/career major
- Transition plan (if applicable)
- Case notes on progress

Work-based Learning

- Documentation of structured work experiences or paid employment
- Signed training agreements
- Employer evaluations

- Resume
- Letters of recommendation

School-based Learning

- Transcripts
- Current academic schedule
- Copies of diplomas, certificates

Final Placement and Follow-up

- Exit planning information
- Completed follow-up forms

Developing a case file system for managing your paperwork takes some time up front, but in the long run it will help your program run more efficiently. When you meet with a student, parent, or employer you can simply retrieve a student file—all the information you need will be easily accessible.

Build Partnerships with School and Community Resources

Identify appropriate school and community resources

One of the first steps in building collaborative services is to identify resources that exist within the school and community. Begin by creating a list of programs and resources in the school and community that offer career planning, vocational training, continuing education, and other related services (e.g., counseling/crisis management). Your list might include many of the programs suggested below as well as others you are aware of in your local community.

Resources Within the High School

- Career planning classes or career information centers
- Professional technical education classes
- Cooperative work experience programs

- School-based enterprises

- Youth apprenticeship programs

Postsecondary and Community Resources

- Business–education compacts

- Federal, state, or local youth training programs

- Rehabilitation agencies and organizations

- Registered apprenticeship programs

- Community college programs

The actual agencies, programs, and resources you target should be determined *by the interests and needs of your students*. For example, assume that while identifying career interests you learn that several students are interested in horticulture and landscaping. Through your knowledge of school resources you know that the high school science teacher is interested in creating applied field experiences for students in her Earth sciences class. The teacher responsible for teaching agriculture and horticulture to vocational education students acquired materials for building greenhouses from a nursery the year before but hasn't had time to build them or get bedding materials. You have the ingredients for a great partnership that will benefit your students and many others.

Share information with existing programs

Once you have created a list of potential resources, the next step is to share information with staff in these school and community programs. Make an on-site visit to the programs. Take the time to ask questions about the specific services and/or training offered as well as any eligibility criteria. This is also a time to share information about your program. These initial discussions will lay the groundwork for future collaborative efforts.

Determine opportunities for collaboration

Once you have a basic understanding of the resources available to your program, staff can begin to develop working relationships with these programs. Begin by focusing on a concrete activity or project that serves the interests of both programs. For example, the summer might be an opportune time to collaborate with a local summer youth employment program. One YTP site was able to create a summer program that integrated academic and occupational learning, using both classroom and community training. In this arrangement, the YTP staff developed community job sites and provided intensive job training and support. The federal basic skills and job training program was responsible for the academic component, and federal funds were used to cover wages for the students. By combining resources, the program was able to provide school-to-work services to at-risk, disadvantaged, and special education students.

EVALUATING STUDENT AND PROGRAM OUTCOMES

Evaluation activities should be embedded into every component of your program. When incorporated into program management strategies, evaluation information can provide essential feedback on a program's implementation and its impact on students, the school, and community. Effective evaluation, however, relies on mechanisms for reviewing evaluation results regularly and using this information as a basis for program modifications and public relations activities. This section describes strategies for evaluating and documenting the impact of your school-to-work program and using this information for program monitoring and marketing.

Develop an Evaluation Plan for the Program

Identify program objectives

One of the most important steps to collecting useful evaluation information is to identify the purposes or uses for the information you will be collecting, the individuals or groups who are the primary audience or users of the information, and the questions you want answered by the information you collect. Attempting to collect evaluation information without attending to this important first step is as foolish as embarking on a cross-country trip with no idea of where you want to go and no map to help you get there.

Identifying evaluation purposes, audiences, and questions should begin with a clear understanding of the most important objectives of your school-to-work program. Clear program objectives provide a guide for organizing your evaluation information. It goes without saying, of course, that clear program objectives also help you deliver more effective, focused services. According to school-to-work legislation and literature, the overall purpose of school-to-work programs is to prepare all students for work and further education and help them enter first jobs in high-skill, high-wage careers. How will your program fulfill this mission statement? This global purpose statement could be translated into a variety of program objectives. At least some of the following types of objectives are possible. Regardless of the objectives you choose, staff should be actively involved in identifying these objectives:

- To improve students' academic and occupational skills related to a target business or industry.

- To provide students with comparable or better skills than entry-level employees in a targeted business or industry.

- To help students stay in and complete high school.

- To place program graduates into career-related postsecondary training.

Identify evaluation purposes, audiences, and questions

We've already indicated that the two general evaluation purposes of concern in this chapter are program monitoring and program marketing. Program monitoring is defined as using evaluation information to determine how well a program and its components are working to achieve intended outcomes. This information should be incorporated into program management procedures in such a way that necessary changes can be identified and discussed by staff and improvements made accordingly. From this definition it is obvious that a primary audience for program monitoring information are the program staff. Other possible users of this information might be school district administrators or funding agency staff if the program is supported by external grant funds. Program marketing is public relations, advertising, and publicity. In short, it is sharing the good news about your program's impact on students, the school, and the community with parents, school staff, and community members. These constituents become the intended users of this information.

Evaluation information on student demographics, experiences, and outcomes can serve both monitoring and marketing purposes. Table 5.1 provides examples of evaluation questions in these areas. To the extent possible, program staff and key administrators should be involved in identifying

Table 5.1
Sample Evaluation Questions

Type of information	Major evaluation questions
Student Demographics	✔ What are the demographic characteristics of the students served by the program? ✔ What barriers to success do the students experience?
Student Outcomes at Time of Program Exit	✔ What is the employment status of students at the time of program exit (e.g., wages, hours, benefits) ✔ What percentage of students obtain their completion document by the time they exit the program? ✔ What percentage of students enter postsecondary education or further training upon leaving the program? ✔ How do outcomes for program participants compare to those of nonparticipants?
Postprogram Outcomes	✔ What is the employment status of students 1 year (or 6 months or 2 years) after leaving the program? ✔ What percent of students completed their postsecondary training 1 year (or 6 months or 2 years) after leaving the program? ✔ What kinds of additional support services do students need to successfully transition from school to adult life? ✔ How do outcomes for program participants compare to those of nonparticipants?

evaluation questions. The ways in which these evaluation questions might be used for program monitoring and marketing are described later in this chapter. At this point in the process, it is important to identify the critical questions that relate to the objectives of your program and that can help you evaluate the extent to which these objectives are being accomplished.

Develop procedures and forms for collecting student outcome information

To the extent possible, the procedures and forms used for program evaluation should also be useful for service delivery purposes. Nothing is more frustrating and troublesome for program staff than to have to complete evaluation forms as an activity separate and unrelated to the documentation already required for service delivery. As much as possible, try to create one set of forms and activities that can serve both purposes. Local YTP sites in Oregon use an evaluation system that links service delivery and evaluation activities. YTP staff use a four-step process to collect information on students. These steps coincide with critical service delivery events.

Evaluation of student experiences and outcomes in the YTP is accomplished by local sites through four basic forms: Entry, Update, Exit, and Follow-up. The Entry form collects information on student demographics and barriers, and employment and education status at entry. This form is completed during the intake process when staff interview students. The information documented on this form is also used during the screening and planning process with students. A copy of the YTP Entry form is included in Appendix 5.9. The Update form collects basic information on the employment and educational experiences of students while they are in the program. This form is completed as part of a 6-month review that staff conduct with students. The 6-month review provides a more formal opportunity for students and staff to assess students' experiences, accomplishments, and progress toward goals. A copy of the YTP Update form is included in Appendix 5.10. The Exit form collects basic information on a student's employment and education status at the time of program exit, the goals the student accomplished through the program, and any needs that remain to be addressed. The use of the Exit form as part of the Exit planning interview was described in Chapter 4, and a copy of the YTP Exit form is included in Appendix 4.2. Finally, as described in Chapter 4, the Follow-up form collects basic information on postprogram status and need for additional services in several areas. This form is used as part of the check in that staff conduct with students every 6 months for the first 2 years after they leave the program. A copy of the Follow-up form currently used by YTP sites is included in Appendix 4.4.

Using the YTP forms as models, customize evaluation forms and procedures to meet the specific needs of your program. At minimum, we recommend you collect information on students at program entry, exit and during follow-up. Avoid the temptation to collect all of the information that is potentially interesting to your program and intended users. Collect the minimal information necessary to achieve your purposes. Also we recommend that you use a consistent format for data collection across forms to allow for comparison at different points in time. For example, if you are interested in collecting information on employment indices (e.g., hour worked per week, hourly wage) make sure to ask these questions the same way across all relevant forms. Without this consistency it will be almost impossible to know whether changes in outcomes are real or an artifact of the way you collected the information. Finally, to the extent possible, consider creating a database for your information using one of the many commercially available software programs. If no one on your staff has experience with these programs, consider working with someone in the computer department of your high school, community college, or university.

Use Information for Program Monitoring and Marketing

Program monitoring and improvement

Program staff will be the primary audience for program monitoring information. Summarize information on the evaluation questions targeted by the program in a manner that allow staff to answer the general question, "Is the program helping students achieve intended outcomes?" The complete set of information collected on students can be analyzed and summarized in several ways to help you answer this general question. Using the sample questions in Table 5.1, for example, information on student outcomes (e.g., percent obtaining completion documents, percent entering full-time career-related employment) can be summarized and compared to nonparticipating students.

It is also possible to explore questions for different groups of students. For example, if gender is documented at program entry and type of employment/education services received in the program are monitored through formal updates, it is possible to explore whether young women and men are equally likely to participate in job training that is related to identified career goals. Or if student at-risk status is documented at program entry, it is possible to examine whether program participants who were identified as at-risk obtain completion documents or achieve employment outcomes comparable to non-at-risk participants. The extent to which all students are benefitting from the program is a critical program monitoring issue. Of course, if services are structured to meet students' individual needs, then students will not receive identical services. However, if your review of evaluation information reveals that students who share some common characteristic (e.g., gender, at-risk status) experience generally poorer outcomes *as a group*, then staff should explore whether these outcomes are related to differential experiences in the program.

So what do you do if evaluation information reveals that participants in general, or subgroups of participants, are not achieving outcomes at a level acceptable to staff? Examine the opportunities provided by the program and the actual experiences of students in the program. Meet with former and current students, individually or in groups, and seek their perceptions of the reasons for the outcomes they have experienced. Find out their opinions of the availability and quality of the opportunities they had in the program. Also, consider collecting information from parents, employers, and community partners. Consumers of your services can provide you with valuable feedback to help improve the program. Finally, examine the ways in which staff are spending their time. Is there a relationship between lack of attention to a particular area of service delivery and student outcomes in that area? We described earlier in this chapter how staff in one YTP site in Oregon discovered upon examination of staff activity logs that little time was being spent in job development, and that this was directly related to their frustration with the limited job training experiences of participants. Good programs recognize that monitoring and improvement is a continual process, and they take active steps to incorporate evaluation information into this process.

Program marketing

Information on student outcomes can also be used as part of an overall marketing effort. A few well-formatted charts or professionally designed reports documenting student outcomes can go a long way toward spreading the word about the impact of your program. Your team will need to create a plan for marketing the program based on the unique needs and strengths of your site. You should spend some time up-front defining the specific audience(s) for your marketing campaign, as well as the outcomes you intend to achieve. As part of your planning process, consult with the school district representative who has responsibility for public relations. This individual can help your team decide who else might be an appropriate community connection. Presentations to the school board, the Chamber of Commerce, or public service clubs will help create new networks and public support for the program.

Information on student outcomes can be incorporated into a variety of marketing materials, including brochures, program overviews, newsletters, or program reports. A newsletter can be a great marketing tool if staff have the interest, ability, and time to continue it. You can use a newsletter to keep employers and community agency staff up to date on the services you provide. Be creative as you think of ways to incorporate student outcome information into your marketing materials. Pictures of students on the job or short vignettes describing student success stories bring the program alive.

Once you have developed your materials you can begin your outreach activities within the school and community. The team should delegate marketing responsibilities according to team members' individual strengths. One team member may be confident and enthusiastic about making presentations to groups of employers or other interested professionals. Another may feel more comfortable using the phone or writing letters of introduction. A program coordinator will normally assume the role for much of the outreach because of his or her familiarity with the schools and community, but other school-to-work staff can also play significant marketing roles, especially in the context of their day-to-day interactions with employers and other community service providers.

One final note about your marketing plan. Make sure that your marketing efforts include working with key school and community leaders to develop the administrative support needed for maintaining the program. Administrative support is one of the most crucial ingredients for ensuring the long-term success of the program. Your team should provide information and develop relationships with building principals, district administrative staff, and school board members, as well as local and state agency staff. These key people need to be informed about school-to-work services and student outcomes. With their support and vision for the future, your program can become a permanent resource for students in transition.

APPENDIX 5.1
JOB DESCRIPTION: YTP TEACHER–COORDINATOR

General Administrative Functions

1. Participate in fiscal planning and management activities associated with school district budgets.

2. Work collaboratively with the school district Personnel Department in hiring, supervising, and evaluating Transition Specialist(s).

3. Participate in writing applications for funding of the program.

4. Communicate regularly with school district administrators, building level personnel, parents, students, and community partners concerning the status of program.

Program Management

5. Coordinate activities associated with the recruitment and screening of student participants, including procedures necessary for determining eligibility for students receiving services from community agencies.

6. Coordinate activities associated with transition planning for students.

7. Coordinate and participate in the implementation of school and community-based instructional programs related to students' career interests and transition plans.

8. Coordinate and participate in the implementation of work-based learning options for students.

9. Establish and coordinate a system for providing follow-up services to participants.

10. Establish and coordinate procedures that insure effective case management of participants by Transition Specialists and documentation of all program activities.

11. Establish and coordinate procedures for evaluating the effectiveness of the program from the perspectives of relevant stakeholders, including: students, parents, employers, schools, and collaborating community agencies.

12. Establish and maintain effective partnerships with other school and community programs providing employment, continuing education, and transition services.

APPENDIX 5.2
JOB DESCRIPTION: YTP TRANSITION SPECIALIST

Student Recruitment/Career Planning

1. Participate in activities related to the recruitment of potential participants.
2. Help students complete the eligibility determination process for any community agencies providing collaborative services.
3. Gather and organize information that is useful for transition planning.
4. When appropriate, attend transition planning meetings with student participants.

Job Training/Employer Recruitment

5. Under the supervision of the Teacher–Coordinator, implement a system for disseminating program information to employers.
6. Maintain and update a system for contacting employers.
7. Analyze work sites and match student participants as deemed appropriate by the Teacher–Coordinator.
8. Provide structured training at community job sites consistent with each student's targeted career goals.
9. Collect data as necessary to document students' progress on the job.

Program Management

10. Provide one-to-one assistance to students in the delivery of instruction for academic, vocational, independent living, and personal–social content areas.
11. Provide support to student participants as deemed necessary by the team.
12. Provide follow-up support for students.
13. Maintain an accurate case file on each student participant.
14. Participate in all team meetings.

APPENDIX 5.3
TEAM ACTION PLAN

Meeting Date _____   Meeting Location _____

Participants:

1. _____   3. _____

2. _____   4. _____

Presenter	Agenda Item	Time	Decision/Action	Responsible Party	Timeline

APPENDIX 5.4
ACTIVITY LOG

Name/Title _____ Month _____

This form is designed to document weekly activities and hours spent by school-to-work staff. The sections of the form are described below:

Recruitment: recruiting, screening, and intake
Career Planning: planning to develop career goals
Employment: job placement, training or monitoring; other work-based learning activities
Instruction: school-based learning activities

Follow-up: exit planning; follow-up support
Program Management: staff meetings, program evaluation activities
Student Support: progress reviews; case coordination activities; crisis management activities

Week of	Total Hours	Recruitment	Career Planning	Employment	Instruction	Follow-up	Program Mgmt	Student Support	Comments

APPENDIX 5.5
STUDENT APPLICATION FORM

Name _____ Date _____

Address/Phone _____

Name of Parent or Guardian _____

Work History

List any paid jobs you have held in the past year:

Employer	Job title/duties	Wage	Start date	End date

List any unpaid, school-based or volunteer work experiences you have had in the last year:

Employer	Job title/duties	Start date	End date

What kind of job are you interested in finding right now? _____

What type of transportation will you use to get back and forth from work?

_____

What are your career goals? _____

_____

(Continues)

School History

Current grade _____ Current or last school attended_____

What subjects in school do you like the most? _____

_____

Do you plan to get further training/education after high school?

_____

Living Arrangements

Where are you living now?

_____

Where would you like to live after you finish school?

_____

Recreational Interests

What do you like to do for fun? (hobbies, sports, etc.) _____

_____

Other Information

What are a few of your personal strengths?

1._____

2._____

Why are you interested in this program? _____

_____

APPENDIX 5.6
NOMINATION FORM

Referred by: _____ Date: _____

Position/Agency: _____

Personal Information

Student name: _____ SSN: _____

Address: _____

City: _____ Zip:_____ Phone: _____

Date of Birth: _____ Age: _____

Why is this student being referred to the program? _____

_____

Vocational Considerations

Please list nominee's vocational skills and interests.

Skills   **Interests/goals**

_____   _____

_____   _____

_____   _____

_____   _____

In your opinion, is this nominee motivated to obtain competitive employ-ment? Why or why not?

_____

_____

_____

_____

_____

(Continues)

Special Considerations

Is nominee currently in school? ☐ Yes ☐ No

If yes, does nominee have a current Individual Education Plan (IEP)?
☐ Yes ☐ No

Has nominee been adjudicated? ☐ Yes ☐ No

If yes, describe the reasons for adjudication. Please be specific.

_____

_____

_____

_____

Does the nominee currently use drugs or alcohol?
☐ Yes ☐ No ☐ Don't know

If yes, is the nominee participating in a drug or alcohol rehabilitation program?
☐ Yes ☐ No

How actively involved and supportive are the nominees's parents with his/her current school program (e.g. attendance at parent conferences, follow through on school-to-home communications regarding homework or discipline)?

☐ Very supportive/consistent ☐ Somewhat *un*supportive/ *in*consistent

☐ Somewhat supportive/consistent ☐ Very *un*supportive/*in*consistent

Please describe any other social support issues that you believe might positively or negatively affect this student's ability to work in a paid competitive job in the community.

_____

_____

Please use the back of this form if you would like to give us any other information that will help us provide services. Thank you for your help.

APPENDIX 5.7
RELEASE OF INFORMATION

> To our participants: We can help you better when we are able to work with other agencies that know you and your family. By signing this form, you are giving permission for these organizations to share information about your situation.

Student name: _____ SSN: _____

I authorize the following individuals or agencies:

- [ ] Centerville School District
- [ ] Bland County Mental Health
- [ ] Children's Services Division
- [ ] Bland County Dept. of Youth Services
- [ ] Private Counselor (specify):
- [ ] Other involved agencies (specify):

- [ ] Centerville Community College
- [ ] Vocational Rehabilitation
- [ ] Social Security

to provide information to: The ABC Program, **including records of:**

[ ] Yes	[ ] No	Family History
[ ] Yes	[ ] No	Employment/Unemployment
[ ] Yes	[ ] No	Educational Reports
[ ] Yes	[ ] No	Alcohol/Drug Treatment
[ ] Yes	[ ] No	Mental Health Services
[ ] Yes	[ ] No	Medical/Psychiatric Treatment
[ ] Yes	[ ] No	Other, as listed:_____

I agree that the agencies and individuals listed above may share and exchange information about my family and my circumstances. [ ] Yes [ ] No
This permission is good for 1 year or until: _____

I may cancel this at any time, but I understand that the cancellation will not affect any information that was released prior to cancellation. I understand that information about my case is confidential and protected by state and federal law. I approve the release of this information. I understand what this agreement means. I am signing on my own accord and have not been pressured to do so.

_____   _____
(Signature)   (Date)

_____   _____
(Staff Signature)   (Date)

APPENDIX 5.8
CASE NOTE FORM

Student Name_____ School_____

Date	Staff Initials	Services Provided	Issues/Comments

APPENDIX 5.9
ENTRY FORM

Name: _____ Date of Report: ___/___/___

Demographic Information:

Name:_____ Gender: ☐ Male ☐ Female
Date of Birth ___/___/___ Social Security #_____
Primary Disability:_____ Secondary Disability _____

Ethnic Status:

1. Caucasian   3. Hispanic   5. Native American
2. African-American   4. Asian/Pacific Islander

Current Status and Barriers:

1. What is the student's current educational status?

Status and Type of Classes	Location of Program
1. Not Enrolled 2. Currently dropped out of school 3. Taking classes for a high school diploma 4. Taking classes for GED 5. Classes for adult basic ed./remedial educ. 6. Life skills classes 7. Academic/vocational classes for postsecondary degree or certificate 8. Vocational skill training/Job Corp 9. Other _____	1. High School 2. Community College 3. 4-yr College or University 4. Voc. training facility/Job Corp 5. Other _____

2. Was the student identified as at risk of dropping out of a secondary education program? ☐ Yes ☐ No

3. What type of completion document did the student have upon referral?
   a. None   e. Vocational certificate
   b. High school diploma   f. A.A. degree
   c. GED   g. Other _____
   d. Graduation certificate

(Continues)

4. What is the student's current living status?
   a. Alone
   b. With parents/family
   c. With spouse/partner
   d. With roommates
   e. Vocational/residential training facility
   f. Other _____

5. What is this student's current employment status?
   a. Not employed
   b. Unpaid work experience placement
   c. Working part-time (< 35 hours/week)
   d. Working full-time (35+ hours/week)

Record all job information in the table on the next page.

6. What are the major barriers to success for this student? (Circle all that apply)
   a. No prior job experience
   b. Unable to maintain jobs
   c. Poor independent living skills
   d. Poor social skills
   e. No means of transportation
   f. Unstable living situation
   g. Difficult family circumstances
   h. History of absenteeism or suspension from school
   i. History of dropping out of school
   j. Prior arrest/jail time
   k. Substance abuse
   l. Previous/current pregnancy
   m. Parenting responsibilities
   n. Other _____

Employer	Job title/ duties	Start date	End date	Hourly wage (enter wage or circle one)	Hrs. per week	Benefits (circle all that apply)	Reason for termination
				1. Wage:$_____ 2. Unpaid work exp. 3. Salary + room or board		1. None 2. Vacation 3. Sick time 4. Medical 5. Dental 6. Retirement	1. Fired 2. Laid off 3. Quit 4. School/ temp job ended
				1. Wage:$_____ 2. Unpaid work exp. 3. Salary + room or board		1. None 2. Vacation 3. Sick time 4. Medical 5. Dental 6. Retirement	1. Fired 2. Laid off 3. Quit 4. School/ temp job ended

APPENDIX 5.10
UPDATE FORM

Name: _____ SSN# _____ Date of Report: ___/___/___

Update Report #: (circle one)   #1   #2   #3   #4   #5   #6

1. What is the student's current educational status?

Status and Type of Classes	Location of Program
1. Not Enrolled 2. Currently dropped out of school 3. Taking classes for a high school diploma 4. Taking classes for GED 5. Classes for adult basic ed./remedial educ. 6. Life skills classes 7. Academic/vocational classes for postsecondary degree or certificate 8. Vocational skill training/Job Corp 9. Other _____	1. High School 2. Community College 3. 4-yr College or University 4. Voc. training facility/Job Corp 5. Other _____

2. What type of completion document has the student received since the last report?

   a. None
   b. High school diploma
   c. GED
   d. Graduation certificate
   e. Vocational certificate
   f. A.A. degree
   g. Other _____

3. What is this student's current employment status?

   a. Not employed
   b. Unpaid work experience placement
   c. Working part-time (< 35 hours/week)
   d. Working full-time (35+ hours/week)

Record all job information in the table on the next page.

(Continues)

Employer	Job title/duties	Start date	End date	Hourly wage (enter wage or circle one)	Hrs. per week	Benefits (circle all that apply)	Reason for termination
				1. Wage:$_____ 2. Unpaid work exp. 3. Salary + room or board		1. None 2. Vacation 3. Sick time 4. Medical 5. Dental 6. Retirement	1. Fired 2. Laid off 3. Quit 4. School/temp job ended
				1. Wage:$_____ 2. Unpaid work exp. 3. Salary + room or board		1. None 2. Vacation 3. Sick time 4. Medical 5. Dental 6. Retirement	1. Fired 2. Laid off 3. Quit 4. School/temp job ended

CHAPTER 6

· ·

Final Thoughts

· ·

Children must have at least one person who believes in them. It could be a counselor, a teacher, a preacher, a friend. It could be you. You never know when a little love, a little support, will plant a small seed of hope.

(EDELMAN, 1992, P. 83)

It simply makes no difference how good the rhetoric is or even how good the intentions are; if there is little or no trust, there is no foundation for permanent success. Only basic goodness gives life to technique. To focus on technique is like cramming your way through school. You sometimes get by, perhaps even get good grades, but you don't pay the price day in and day out, you never achieve true mastery of the subjects you study or develop an educated mind. Did you ever consider how ridiculous it would be to try to cram on a farm—to forget to plant in the spring, play all summer and then cram in the fall to bring in the harvest? The price must be paid and the process followed. You always reap what you sow; there is no shortcut. This principle is also true, ultimately, in human behavior, in human relationships.

(COVEY, 1989, P. 21–22)

Planting seeds of hope. Trust not technique. Commitment to the process over time. Reaping what you sow. We can't think of four statements that better summarize the promise that school-to-work programs hold for youth with special needs.

At its very core, the school-to-work reform movement is about hope. Hope for a better future for all youth, but especially those youth who have not benefitted as much or as well from the traditional high school curriculum. Hope that school-to-work programs will bring meaning to the educational enterprise for these youth, and that this will encourage them to stay in and complete school. And, finally, hope that by doing so these youth will acquire solid academic and occupational skills that will prepare them for further learning, better paying jobs, and a brighter future.

This book and others like it offer ideas and strategies for building school-to-work programs that can fulfill these hopeful aspirations. But, as we said at the very beginning of this book, building quality school-to-work programs is not ultimately about having the best techniques. Quality school-to-work programs are built through the creative, dedicated efforts of people who are keenly aware of students' needs and strongly committed to providing programs and resources that meet those needs. Denise Bissonnette (1994), in her book on creative job development, identifies eight character traits of the entrepreneurial job developer that we believe apply equally well to creative, dedicated school-to-work practitioners. We offer them, and short explanations of their meaning for school-to-work services, for your consideration.

- *You are on the path of right livelihood and have a mission.* Your work should be a focus of great passion. It should be consistent with your interests, talents, and personal values. It should be a source of learning, growth, and development.

- *You treat job development (or the school-to-work services you provide) as an art as well as a science.* The materials you have to work with include your students, the community, and the strategies you know so well. These materials cannot be combined in formulaic fashion. Use your style, personality, values, principles, intelligence, and imagination to create new possibilities.

- *You choose to operate out of the abundance mentality rather than the scarcity mentality.* The scarcity mentality breeds scarcity, the abundance mentality breeds abundance. The abundance mentality means giving unselfishly to meet another's needs. It encourages us to work in the best interests of everyone rather than being concerned about receiving reward, credit, or ownership.

- *You believe in your power to effect change.* We can choose to accept conditions as they exist or accept responsibility for changing them. The first option changes nothing. The second option changes everything.

- *You are willing to be a leader.* One of the more powerful ways of leading is through the example of our everyday conviction of purpose and our commitment to excellence and integrity.

- *You are willing to question the status quo and seek creative solutions to problems.* Seeking creative solutions to problems requires a willingness to tread new, sometimes uncharted, territory. It requires that we sometimes forsake familiar, proven notions about what people can and cannot do, and operate from a spirit of exploration and discovery.

- *You aspire to reach your full potential and refuse to settle for less than what is possible.* Holding these values for ourselves makes it much easier to impart them to our students.

- *You gladly remain a beginner and a fresh learner.* We can always learn more no matter how much we already know. School-to-work personnel should never stop questioning their goals, expectations, and methods.

If quality school-to-work programs are built by people with character traits such as these, then they are *sustained* on the trust that participants and partners have for one another, and on their mutual commitment to the process over time. As the chapter opening epigraph from Stephen Covey's (1989) *The 7 Habits of Highly Effective People* suggests, quality programs and human success stories follow the law of the harvest. We cannot cram for a quality program or successful students any more than we can cram for a bumper crop a week before the harvest. We must be willing to invest the time and resources required to plant seeds of hope in our students, and nurture their growth and development through trust and commitment to the process. It is then only a matter of time before we reap bountiful harvests from what has been sown.

References

Bailey, T., & Merritt, D. (1993). *The school-to-work transition and youth apprenticeship: Lessons from the U.S. experience.* New York: Manpower Demonstration Research.

Bennett, W. J. (Ed.). (1993). *The book of virtues.* New York: Simon & Shuster.

Benz, M. R., & Kochhar, C. A. (1996). School-to-work opportunities for all students: A position statement of the Division on Career Development and Transition. *Career Development for Exceptional Individuals,19*, 31–48.

Benz, M. R., Lindstrom, L., & Halpern, A. S. (1995). Mobilizing local communities to improve transition services. *Career Development for Exceptional Individuals, 18*, 21–32.

Benz, M. R., Yovanoff, P., & Doren, B. (1997). School-to-work components that predict postschool success for students with and without disabilities. *Exceptional Children, 63*, 151–165.

Bissonnette, D. (1994). *Beyond traditional job development: The art of creating opportunity.* Chatsworth, CA: Milt Wright.

Canfield, J. (1993). Follow your dream. In J. Canfield & M. V. Hansen (Eds.), *Chicken soup for the soul: 101 stories to open the heart and rekindle the spirit* (pp. 207–208). Deerfield Beach, FL: Health Communications.

Carnegie Council on Adolescent Development. (1995). *Great transitions: Preparing adolescents for a new century.* New York: Carnegie.

Choy, S. P. (1994). School-to-work opportunities: Issues in state and local governance. In N. G. Stacey (Ed.), *School-to-work: What does research say about it?* (pp. 57–76). Washington, DC: U.S. Department of Education, Office of Educational Research and Improvement, Office of Research.

Choy, S. P., Alt, M. N., & Henke, R. R. (1994). Profile of the target populations for the school-to-work transition initiatives. In N. G. Stacey (Ed.), *School-to-work: What does research say about it?* (pp. 97–130). Washington, DC: U.S. Department of Education, Office of Educational Research and Improvement, Office of Research.

Covey, S. R. (1989). *The 7 habits of highly effective people: Restoring the character ethic.* New York: Simon & Shuster.

Dryfoos, J. G. (1990). *Adolescents at risk: Prevalence and prevention.* New York: Oxford University Press.

Edelman, M. W. (1992). *The measure of our success: A letter to my children and yours*. Boston: Beacon Press.

Fardig, D. G., Algozzine, R. F., Schwartz, S. E., Hensel, J. W., & Westling, D. L. (1985). Postsecondary vocational adjustment of rural mildly handicapped students. *Exceptional Children, 52*, 115–121.

Freedman, M., & Baker, R. (1995). *Workplace mentoring for youth: Context, issues, strategies*. Washington, DC: National Institute for Work and Learning, Academy for Educational Development.

Goals 2000: Educate America Act of 1994 [On-line]. Available: http://www.ed.gov/legislation/GOALS2000/TheACT/

Goldberger, S., Kazis, R., & O'Flanagan, M. K. (1994). *Learning through work: Designing and implementing quality worksite learning for high school students*. New York: Manpower Demonstration Research.

Grubb, W. N. (1994, August). True reform or tired retread? Questions to ask about school-to-work programs. *Education Week, 68*, 54.

Halpern, A. S. (1993). Quality of life as a conceptual framework for evaluating transition outcomes. *Exceptional Children, 59*, 486–498.

Halpern, A. S. (1994). The transition of youth with disabilities to adult life: A position statement of the Division on Career Development and Transition. *Career Development for Exceptional Individuals, 17*, 115–124.

Halpern, A. S., Herr, C. M., Wolf, N. K., Doren, B., Johnson, M. B., & Lawson, J. D. (1997). NEXT S.T.E.P.: Student transition and educational planning. Austin, TX: PRO-ED.

Hamilton, S. E., & Hamilton, M. A. (1994). *Opening career paths for youth: What can be done? Who can do it?* Cornell Youth and Work Program, Cornell University, American Youth Policy Forum, Jobs for the Future.

Hasazi, S., Gordon, L. R., & Roe, C. A. (1985). Factors associated with the employment status of handicapped youth exiting high school from 1979 to 1983. *Exceptional Children, 51*, 455–469.

Heal, L. W., Copher, J. I., & Rusch, F. R. (1990). Inter-agency agreements (IAAs) among agencies responsible for the transition education of students with handicaps for secondary schools to postsecondary settings. *Career Development for Exceptional Individuals, 13*, 121–127.

Horn, W., O'Donnell, J., & Vitulano, A. (1983). Long-term follow-up studies of learning disabled persons. *Journal of Learning Disabilities, 16*, 542–555.

Johnson, J. R., & Rusch, F. R. (1993). Secondary special education and transition services: Identification and recommendations for future research and demonstration. *Career Development for Exceptional Individuals, 16*, 1–18.

Kyle, R. M. J. (1995). *School-to-work transition and its role in the systemic reform of education*. Washington, DC: National Institute for Work and Learning, Academy for Educational Development.

Liontos, L. B. (1992). *At-risk families and schools: Becoming partners*. Eugene, OR: ERIC Clearinghouse on Educational Management, University of Oregon. (ERIC/CEM Accession No. EA 023 283)

Lombard, R. C., Hazelkorn, M. N., & Miller, R. J. (1995). Special populations and Tech-Prep: A national study of state policies and practices. *Career Development for Exceptional Individuals, 18*, 145–156.

Marder, C., & D'Amico, R. (1992). *How well are youth with disabilities really doing? A comparison of youth with disabilities and youth in general.* Menlo Park, CA: SRI International.

McNeil, P. W., & Kulick, C. D. (1995). *Employers' role in school-to-work opportunities.* Washington, DC: National Institute for Work and Learning, Academy for Educational Development.

Mendel, R. (1994). *The American school-to-career movement: A background paper for policymakers and foundation officers.* Washington, DC: American Youth Policy Forum.

Mithaug, D. E., Horiuchi, C. N., & Fanning, P. N. (1985). A report on the Colorado statewide follow-up survey of special education students. *Exceptional Children, 51*, 397–404.

Mithaug, D. E., Martin, J. E., Agran, M., & Rusch, F. R. (1988). *Why special education graduates fail: How to teach them to succeed.* Colorado Springs, CO: Ascent.

Moore, M. T., & Waldman, Z. (1994). Opportunities or obstacles? A map of federal legislation related to the school-to-work initiative. In N. G. Stacey (Ed.), *School-to-work: What does research say about it?* (pp. 131–184). Washington, DC: U.S. Department of Education, Office of Educational Research and Improvement, Office of Research.

National Center on Education and the Economy. (1990). *America's choice: High skills or low wages.* Rochester, NY: Author.

National Organization on Disability. (1994). *N.O.D. Survey of Americans with Disabilities.* Washington, DC: Author.

National Transition Network (1994, Summer). *Policy update: Youth with disabilities and the School-to-Work Opportunities Act of 1994.* Minneapolis, MN: Author.

Norman, M. E., & Bourexis, P. S. (1995). *Including students with disabilities in school-to-work opportunities.* Washington, DC: Council of Chief State School Officers.

Orr, M. T. (1995). *Evaluating school-to-work transition.* Washington, DC: National Institute for Work and Learning, Academy for Educational Development.

Paris, K. A. (1994). *A leadership model for planning & implementing change for school-to-work transition.* Madison, WI: University of Wisconsin, Center on Education and Work.

Pauly, E., Kopp, H., & Haimson, J. (1994). *Home-grown lessons: Innovative programs linking work and high school.* New York: Manpower Demonstration Research.

Rogers, A., Hubbard, S., Charner, I., Fraser, B. S., & Horne, R. (1995). *Learning from experience: A cross-case comparison of school-to-work transition reform initiatives.* Washington, DC: National Institute for Work and Learning, Academy for Educational Development.

Rusch, F. R., Kohler, P. D., & Hughes, C. (1992). An analysis of OSERS'-sponsored secondary special education and transitional services research. *Career Development for Exceptional Individuals, 15*, 121–143.

Schultz, J. B. (1994). Facts of life: Secondary school course readies teens for everyday adult responsibilities. *Vocational Education Journal, 69*(4), 19–21, 41.

Seuss, D. (1990). *Oh, the places you'll go!* New York: Random House.

Siegel, S., Robert, M., Greener, K., Meyer, G., Halloran, W., & Gaylord-Ross, R. (1993). *Career ladders for challenged youths in transition from school to adult life.* Austin, TX: PRO-ED.

Terkel, S. (1974). *Working: People talk about what they do all day and how they feel about what they do*. New York: Random House.

U.S. Department of Education. (1994). School-to-Work Opportunities Act of 1994 [On-line]. Available: http://www.stw.ed.gov/factsht/act.htm.

U.S. Department of Labor, Education and Training Administration, Office of Work-based Learning. (1992). *School-to-work connections: Formulas for success*. Washington, DC: Author.

U.S. Department of Labor, The Secretary's Commission on Achieving Necessary Skills. (1991). *What work requires of schools*. Washington, DC: U.S. Government Printing Office.

U.S. General Accounting Office. (1991). *Transition from school-to-work: Linking education and work-site training* (HRD 91–105). Washington, DC: U.S. Government Printing Office.

Wagner, M., D'Amico, R., Marder, C., Newman, L., & Blackorby, J. (1992). *What happens next? Trends in postschool outcomes of youths with disabilities: The second comprehensive report from the National Longitudinal Transition Study of Special Education Students*. Menlo Park, CA: SRI International.

Wagner, M., Newman, L., D'Amico, R., Jay, E., Butler-Nalin, P., Marder, C., & Cox, R. (1991). *Youth with disabilities: How are they doing? The first comprehensive report from the National Longitudinal Transition Study of Special Education Students*. Menlo Park, CA: SRI International.

Weinbaum, A., & Rogers, A. M. (1995). *Contextual learning: A critical aspect of school-to-work transition programs*. Washington, DC: National Institute for Work and Learning, Academy for Educational Development.

William T. Grant Foundation. (1988). *The forgotten half: Pathways to success for America's youth and young families* (Final Report). Washington, DC: Author.

Index